PRAISE FOR *STOP SELLING & START LEADING*

"Separately, I've admired Deb Calvert's outstanding sales book and blog and the legendary leadership writings of Kouzes and Posner. Together, they have found a 'chocolate meets peanut butter' combination that is so needed for the sales profession in our current buyer's market and VUCA business environment. They have—through research—validated an approach that has the potential to elevate the sales profession. *Stop Selling & Start Leading* is truly a roadmap for evolving seller behavior to radically transform your organization's sales results."

—**Mike Kunkle,** VP of Sales Transformation Services for
Digital Transformation, Inc., a division of Fast Lane

"The chasm between how buyers want to buy and how salespeople sell is a mile wide and seemingly impossible to cross. Until now. This book sheds much-needed light on how to ditch ineffective old-school selling tactics and adopt the leadership behaviors that buyers crave from today's sellers. Based on eye-popping buyer research and a proven leadership model, the authors present a clear roadmap for navigating the B2B sales process with integrity, credibility, and dignity for a true win-win experience."

—**Julie Hansen,** author of *Sales Presentations for Dummies* and *ACT Like a Sales Pro!,* speaker, founder, Performance Sales and Training

"I'm a long-time fan of Kouzes and Posner's leadership expertise and Calvert's perspective on what it takes to succeed in sales. What a thrill to see them apply these proven leadership principles to professional selling! *Stop Selling & Start Leading* offers a powerful perspective on why sellers who lead well will thrive and then provides clear, practical guidance on how to gain credibility and respect that will move buyers to act. Read. This. Now. to set yourself apart from the typical, ineffective salesperson who is perceived as nothing more than a vendor/supplier."

—**Mike Weinberg,** author of *New Sales. Simplified and Sales Management. Simplified*

"*Stop Selling & Start Leading* is not the normal sales book, which is what makes it so powerful. Too many salespeople think sales is about techniques. High performance selling has little to do with technique; it's all about leadership. It's helping customers solve their problems, aligning the buying group, and helping them mobilize to take action. Great sellers are great leaders—with their customers and within their own organizations. *Stop Selling & Start Leading* is a thoughtful discussion about how salespeople provide this leadership. It focuses on the five practices critical for leadership, providing great case studies and lessons in each practice. Make these practices the core of your approach in providing great sales leadership."

—**Dave Brock,** author, *Sales Manager Survival Guide;* CEO, Partners In EXCELLENCE

"*Stop Selling & Start Leading* shows sellers precisely how to differentiate themselves from the pack and turn customers into clients for life. If you're looking for a way to break out of the traditional sales mode and become a valued member of your client's team, this book gives you the five steps to do exactly that."

—**Kendra Lee,** author of the award-winning books *The Sales Magnet* and *Selling Against the Goal;* president of the KLA Group

"Every leader, sales leader, and individual who wants a successful career in selling should read this book. What you'll discover is the liberating truth, backed by brand-new research that proves leading is the new selling. *Stop Selling & Start Leading* not only reveals new science behind how customers want to be sold, it tells you exactly how to do it. It contains insights that ascend sales process, and it supersedes old-school selling behaviors. For those who truly want the highest levels of success for themselves and their clients, I offer my highest recommendation."

—**James Muir,** CEO, Best Practice International

"In *Stop Selling & Start Leading,* the authors have delivered a beautiful masterpiece that is guaranteed to make you a more effective and respected sales professional."

—**Jeb Blount,** CEO of Sales Gravy and author of *Sales EQ*

"The authors start with a chapter on credibility, which in their view creates the foundation for leadership and selling. That's why their book simply 'rings true.' You won't find an ounce of counterfeit data or advice. Exemplary research illustrated by wise practitioner stories makes for great reading and solid guidance. An instant classic for every B2B seller."

—**Barbara Weaver Smith,** founder and CEO, The Whale Hunters

"In today's world so much about sales focuses on processes, CRMs, and systems, when in reality the most important thing in sales is PEOPLE—always has been and always will. In professional selling PEOPLE buy from PEOPLE. *Stop Selling & Start Leading*'s research with both buyers and sellers provides a treasure trove of information to help salespeople lead and sell more effectively and buyers to once again enjoy the experience—while their companies benefit with improved behaviors and better bottom-line results on both sides."

—**Debbie Mrazek,** founder and president, The Sales Company

"My favorite line in this book is super simple: 'The seller becomes a trusted advisor.' The principles and steps required to achieve that level of buyer confidence are outlined in *Stop Selling & Start Leading*. Read it to make extraordinary sales happen."

—**Tom Hopkins,** author of *How to Master the Art of Selling* and *When Buyers Say No*

"If your customers don't see you as a leader, then they don't need you. The game of selling has changed, and the customer is rewriting the rulebook. Be seen as a leader or you won't be seen at all!"

—**Mark Hunter,** "The Sales Hunter," author of *High-Profit Prospecting*

"The research supporting The Five Practices of Exemplary Leadership® is powerful. Buyers have spoken. They want sellers to stop using old-school sales tactics that make them feel unimportant. The authors clearly outline the behaviors buyers not only want, but so desperately need. Sellers who exhibit them and create value with every conversation will win."

—**Nancy Bleeke,** author of *Conversations That Sell*

"If you are in sales and not happy with your results or simply trying to achieve more, what behaviors are you willing to change? *Stop Selling & Start Leading* is a great read on how sales execs can make simple tweaks in their behaviors that will generate significant results. But it all starts with you taking the first step and reading this book, which I highly recommend."

—**Ron Karr,** author, *Lead, Sell, or Get Out of the Way*

STOP SELLING

&

START LEADING

How to Make *Extraordinary* Sales Happen

JAMES KOUZES

BARRY POSNER

DEB CALVERT

WILEY

Published by The Leadership Challenge, a Wiley Brand
Published simultaneously in Canada.

No part of this publication may be reproduced, stored in a retrieval system, or transmitted in any form or by any means, electronic, mechanical, photocopying, recording, scanning, or otherwise, except as permitted under Section 107 or 108 of the 1976 United States Copyright Act, without either the prior written permission of the publisher, or authorization through payment of the appropriate per-copy fee to the Copyright Clearance Center, Inc., 222 Rosewood Drive, Danvers, MA 01923, 978-750-8400, fax 978-646-8600, or on the Web at www.copyright.com. Requests to the publisher for permission should be addressed to the Permissions Department, John Wiley & Sons, Inc., 111 River Street, Hoboken, NJ 07030, 201-748-6011, fax 201-748-6008, or online at www.wiley.com/go/permissions.

Limit of Liability/Disclaimer of Warranty: While the publisher and author have used their best efforts in preparing this book, they make no representations or warranties with respect to the accuracy or completeness of the contents of this book and specifically disclaim any implied warranties of merchantability or fitness for a particular purpose. No warranty may be created or extended by sales representatives or written sales materials. The advice and strategies contained herein may not be suitable for your situation. You should consult with a professional where appropriate. Neither the publisher nor author shall be liable for any loss of profit or any other commercial damages, including but not limited to special, incidental, consequential, or other damages. Readers should be aware that Internet Web sites offered as citations and/or sources for further information may have changed or disappeared between the time this was written and when it is read.

This publication is designed to provide accurate and authoritative information in regard to the subject matter covered. It is sold with the understanding that the publisher is not engaged in rendering professional services. If legal, accounting, medical, psychological or any other expert assistance is required, the services of a competent professional should be sought.

For general information on our other products and services, please contact our Customer Care Department within the U.S. at 800-956-7739, outside the U.S. at 317-572-3986, or fax 317-572-4002.

Wiley publishes in a variety of print and electronic formats and by print-on-demand. Some material included with standard print versions of this book may not be included in e-books or in print-on-demand. If this book refers to media such as a CD or DVD that is not included in the version you purchased, you may download this material at http://booksupport.wiley.com. For more information about Wiley products, visit www.wiley.com. For more information about The Leadership Challenge, visit www.leadershipchallenge.com

Library of Congress Cataloging-in-Publication Data
Names: Kouzes, James M., author. | Posner, Barry Z., author. | Calvert, Deb, author.
Title: Stop selling and start leading : how to make extraordinary sales happen / James M. Kouzes, Barry Z. Posner, Deb Calvert.
Other titles: Stop selling & start leading
Description: Hoboken : Wiley, 2018. | Includes index. |
Identifiers: LCCN 2017051649 (print) | LCCN 2017054512 (ebook) | ISBN 9781119446323 (epub) | ISBN 9781119446316 (pdf) | ISBN 9781119446286 (hardback)
Subjects: LCSH: Leadership. | Selling.
Classification: LCC HD57.7 (ebook) | LCC HD57.7 .K686 2018 (print) | DDC 658.85--dc23
LC record available at https://lccn.loc.gov/2017051649

Cover design by Wiley

Printed in the United States of America

FIRST EDITION

HB Printing   10 9 8 7 6 5 4 3 2 1
PB Printing   10 9 8 7 6 5 4 3 2 1

CONTENTS

STOP
SELLING

&

START
LEADING

INTRODUCTION: HOW YOU MAKE EXTRAORDINARY SALES HAPPEN

STOP SELLING & START LEADING is a book about how to make more sales. How? Our research shows you can make more sales by abandoning sales-y behaviors buyers resist and replacing them with *leadership* behaviors buyers desire. This book is about the extraordinary things sellers do when they stop pushing people to buy before they're ready, and they start guiding buyers by transforming values into actions, visions into realities, obstacles into innovations, separateness into solidarity, and risks into rewards. *Stop Selling & Start Leading* is about ennobling the sales profession and dignifying buyers, a shift that turns tedious transactions into exciting customer experiences.

This book is focused as much on buyers as it is on sellers, which represents a truth every exemplary leader understands: it's not about you, it's about your constituents—their needs, hopes, dreams, and aspirations—and leaders can't make anything happen all by themselves. Today buyers have enormous power and information and more choices than ever before. They dodge sellers, delay decisions, demand price concessions, and expect more but give less. Buyers scarcely tolerate sellers and often unfairly stereotype them, erecting barriers to entry without giving sellers a fair chance.

Stop Selling & Start Leading is aimed directly at sellers. It's for sellers who work diligently but still struggle to mobilize buyers and meet ever-increasing quotas. It's for sellers who face buyer cynicism, despite their best efforts to differentiate themselves and their sincere intent to help their buyers. This is a book for sellers who are looking for ways to build relationships with buyers and to succeed in reaching mutual goals.

This is also a book about leadership. Leadership is not a formal position or an official place in the organizational hierarchy. Leadership is not a genetic trait or limited by gender, ethnic or racial background, family or social status, appearance, or nationality. Leadership is an observable and learnable set of skills and abilities that is accessible to everyone. Research clearly shows that in the highest performing organizations *leadership is everyone's business*.[1] Similarly, evidence abounds that the most exemplary sellers engage most frequently in the practices of leadership. Leaders, like extraordinary sellers, are change brokers. They are guides who show people the way from where they are now to where they aspire to be in the future. Leaders make extraordinary things happen. We believe you can, too.

When you lay down your old-school selling behaviors and mindset, buyers will see you as something more than the stereotypical fast-talking, high-pressure, know-it-all seller. When you choose, instead, to behave as a leader, buyers will respond favorably. Buyers will want you to lead them to an ideal place.

How do we know what behaviors buyers want to see from sellers? We asked them. Our groundbreaking research with more than five hundred B2B buyers provides a blueprint of behaviors sellers can follow to book more meetings and close more sales. We also asked hundreds of sellers to tell us stories about their own *personal-best experiences* in selling. In story after story, the same behaviors appeared. Sellers succeeded the most when they demonstrated behaviors associated with leadership.

Our research with buyers and sellers is new and reveals some surprising findings; however, the research we'll share about leadership is not new. Long before we asked buyers to tell us what behaviors they wanted to see more frequently from sellers, Jim and Barry started conducting research with leaders from around the world, in every industry and discipline. Their research pinpoints the behaviors exhibited by people when they were at their personal best as leaders—when they made extraordinary things happen. It also shows the impact of these behaviors on constituent engagement. In other words, we know through this research what makes leadership effective. Jim and Barry call this framework The Five Practices of Exemplary Leadership®, and it consists of ten leadership commitments.[2]

The Five Practices gave us a great starting point and foundation for investigating the relationships between sellers and buyers. In our research with buyers, we asked what would happen if sellers exhibited these same leadership behaviors in their relationship with buyers. We also asked how frequently sellers already behave in these ways and how often buyers would ideally like to see these behaviors used by sellers. The findings make a compelling case for a behavioral shift. Sales effectiveness, like leadership effectiveness, can be significantly increased by choosing to behave differently.

We use the terms *buyers, sellers, leaders,* and *behaviors* deliberately throughout this book. *Buyers* is used to represent all people at all phases of the sales cycle, from suspects to prospects to clients. *Sellers* refers to everyone who sells, regardless of role, from Sales Development Rep to Major Accounts Manager. *Leaders* refers to everyone who makes a choice to lead. This word is not intended to suggest a management-level role in the organization. We're using the word *leader* to talk about you, a seller, who decides to utilize the behaviors of exemplary leadership when working with your buyers. Finally, we talk a great deal in this book about *behaviors,* the actions people perform when they are leading. That's because the actions you take matter much more than what you think, feel, say, or intend.

As you read sellers' stories and buyers' comments, you'll get first-hand examples of how to modify your behaviors to be more effective with buyers. You'll see what it means to become an exemplary seller who guides buyers to a better place.

In Chapter One we review shifts in buyer desires and demands. We identify the five buyer preferences that originally led to our hypothesis that sellers would be more successful if they replaced traditional selling behaviors with the behaviors of exemplary leaders. This is where you'll find a deeper dive into the research that proved this hypothesis.

Selling, like leading, is based on relationships with people. To go straight to the core of what people need in order to follow someone *willingly*, we devote Chapter Two to a single characteristic that is the cornerstone of leadership: credibility. It's also the one characteristic that buyers most emphatically told us was lacking in sellers. We describe what it is, why it matters so much, and how buyers assess—beginning with the first encounter—whether a seller has this essential quality.

The ten chapters that follow describe the Ten Commitments of Leadership—the essential behaviors that leaders employ to make extraordinary things happen—and explain what sellers must do to shift their behaviors within each of The Five Practices. Stories from sellers describing their personal bests provide examples of these Ten Commitments in action, and buyers' comments magnify the key points. Evidence from our studies and sellers' reports make the case for adopting these behaviors. Each of these leadership practice sections ends with ideas for you to *Take Action*, suggestions you can implement immediately to liberate the leader inside you. None of the recommendations in this book requires a budget, hierarchical approval, or organization-wide change. All that's required is your commitment and discipline. It's all up to you.

In Chapter Thirteen, we talk more about that choice. Your choice. We call on every seller to be a leader, to rise to the challenge of becoming the leader that buyers are looking for. Sellers shouldn't feel ashamed of the work they do and the profession they represent. You can choose to shed the stereotypes and become a different kind of seller, one who leads with pride and serves as a partner with buyers.

We recommend you first read Chapter One for the background information. As you do, think about the reception you've had from buyers and put yourself in their shoes. Consider the case for changing your behavior. When you're ready to take the plunge, move on to Chapter Two to understand why this behavioral shift is critical. As you proceed through the remaining chapters, look for ways to become a leader with your buyers, with your internal partners, and even with yourself. Even though buyers rank some leadership practices as more important than others, remember that buyers want to see something more or different from sellers in every one of the practices. Each leadership practice and commitment is essential.

Your buyers are eager to see you make these changes. The sales profession needs more people to step into their full leadership potential. The world beyond selling needs leaders, too, in every sector, in every community, in every country. We need extraordinary leadership, and we need people to provide leadership now more than ever. There is so much amazing work yet to do. We need leaders who can ignite and unite us.

When you stop selling and start leading, buyers will respond. You will, too. Becoming a leader is one of the noblest and most energizing things you will ever do. We fervently hope this book will enrich your life and the lives of your buyers, your family, your colleagues, and your community. Are you ready?

James Kouzes
Orinda, California

Barry Posner
Berkeley, California

Deb Calvert
Peculiar, Missouri

March 2018

WHAT IF SELLERS BEHAVED AS LEADERS?

1 | WHEN SELLERS ARE AT THEIR BEST

AMY SPELLMAN MADE A MID-LIFE CAREER CHANGE. She became an insurance agent because she wanted to help people. Amy was excited about the fresh start, income potential, and opportunity to make a difference in people's lives.

Six months later, Amy left sales. For her, the role was unfulfilling despite the higher income. Following up company-generated leads and making cold calls felt like dialing-for-dollars, and calling people multiple times felt like an imposition. Selling in a high-pressure environment meant spending less time helping people in the way she'd envisioned. Instead of feeling supportive, she felt pushy. Instead of enjoying connections with clients, she felt inauthentic, rushed, and slightly manipulative when using sales tactics she had observed and learned from others.[1]

Perhaps you've felt the same way at some time in your sales role. Maybe you've sensed that buyers seem suspicious and guarded when you contact them. Or possibly your friends and family are cynical and question your character and integrity because you are in sales.

REDEFINING THE B2B BUYER EXPERIENCE

The pervasive, negative stereotypes about sellers affect how people initially react to you, even, on occasion, family and friends who know you well. The *Glengarry Glen Ross* and *Wolf of Wall Street* movie personas of sellers are reinforced in real life often enough to put buyers on the defensive. As Amy said, "It didn't feel like I could win. The people I called assumed I was going to take advantage of them. They didn't even give me a chance to show how I would be different." What's a seller to do?

More of the Same Behaviors Results in More of the Same Reactions

Too many sellers simply shrug their shoulders and adopt these stereotypical behaviors. Others defuse buyers' negative perceptions by operating with integrity, the more challenging path to be sure.

For buyers, the challenge is to separate the wheat from the chaff, determining which sellers are trustworthy. An overwhelming refrain from buyers in our study was, as one person said, "All sellers seem to be saying and doing the same things."[2] Sellers, despite their intentions, are failing to behaviorally differentiate themselves.

As buyers become increasingly self-sufficient and more resistant to advances, sellers scramble to find more leads, make more calls, and get in front of more buyers. Engaging in more of the same old sales behaviors exacerbates the problem. All sellers seem the same, because they're all behaving the same way.

Something Different, but What?

There must be another option. Retail researchers Robin Lewis and Michael Dart concluded that winning people's wallets requires delivering "such an awesome connecting experience that they will go out of their way to come to you."[3] "An awesome connecting experience"? Now that's something different in selling! It's a phrase that's more likely to be associated with leadership. Let's break it down.

☑ Awesome.

When we're using the slang definition of *awesome*, it means the sales call is going to be "very impressive." Jaded buyers won't rate even the best selling behaviors as "very impressive." Quality is a weak differentiator that may go completely unnoticed. The dictionary meaning of *awesome* is more applicable: "causing an overwhelming feeling of admiration or respect." Now that's something that would certainly capture a buyer's attention and clearly be differentiating.

Anthony Iannarino, the founder of The Sales Blog, says such a response only comes with genuine caring for your buyer.[4] He believes the power of caring is unmatched and that those who care deeply about their buyers "will stand out from the crowd and be welcomed as trusted, valued partners." Empathy, intimacy, and presence, he asserts, create the caring experience that keep buyers coming back for more.

☑ Connecting.

Connecting, too, aims for differentiation. *Connecting* means joining or linking. To be clear, connecting means much more than a social media link. It involves more than the initial rapport-building you do with prospects. A connection isn't just a name in your CRM. Connections aren't sufficiently made by automation and artificial intelligence (AI). In human interactions, there's a need for *emotional* connection.

Jeb Blount, CEO of Sales Gravy, says the point of connecting in sales is to "win other people over by making them feel that they are the center of your attention, to make them feel significant or important," and then to "nurture a deep emotional connection [because] people buy from people they like, trust, and believe will solve their problems."[5] Buyers want authentic connections, not superficial ones that evaporate when the sale is closed.

> **Sellers must reach buyers by creating genuine and authentic experiences.**

☑ **Experience.**

In ancient times, people traded commodities to survive. As manufacturing expanded, sellers offered variety and quality to distinguish their goods. In time, service became the differentiation between one manufacturer's goods and another's. Today, service is no longer enough. Buyers demand more.

Linda Richardson, who teaches sales and management courses at the Wharton School, asserts that "a huge part of buying for almost all buyers is the experience." She says that "when clients feel you are there for them, they will go out of their way to be there for you." Linda concludes that it's important to be human-focused in creating an experience that creates intimacy with your buyer.[6]

Creating an "awesome connecting experience" is also essential in leadership. After all, where would leaders be without followers; and where would sellers be without buyers? Leadership research and theories have evolved over the years, from a transactional to a transformational perspective, from simply seeing leadership as an exchange between leaders and constituents to thinking about it as a way to foster positive changes for those who follow. Nearly two decades ago, sales and marketing scholars followed suit and began articulating that *experience* is the missing link between sellers and buyers.[7] Sellers must reach buyers by creating genuine and authentic experiences.[8] Experiences aren't manufactured or engineered by sellers or their companies. Rather, a buyer derives personal meaning because of his or her imprint on the interactive experience. The seller's role is to facilitate a highly personalized interaction.

An "awesome connecting experience" is an incredibly high standard. Most B2B sellers focus on goods and services. Buyers react by commoditizing these offerings and focusing on price alone. Striving toward the high standard of an awesome connecting experience is no longer merely optional. It's absolutely essential because buyers are accustomed to it in their B2C shopping experiences.

Lessons from the B2C Customer Experience

Businesses that sell directly to consumers have steadily increased efforts to enhance the customer experience (CX). Consumers have been conditioned to expect an experience that is personal and relevant. This experience, to be entirely satisfying, will involve consumers directly and engage them emotionally. Because buyers are being conditioned to expect this, what's lacking for them in their B2B experiences includes:

> **Experiences resonate and motivate when they touch people's hearts, not just their minds.**

☑ **Direct Involvement.**

In *The Future of Competition: Co-Creating Unique Value with Customers*, the authors predicted that "consumers will migrate to businesses that allow them to be participants in creating what they want."[9] Consumers flock to businesses like Starbucks and Build-A-Bear Workshop for hands-on experiences to create precisely what they want.

☑ **Emotional Engagement.**

Personal involvement requires more than sharing opinions and directing product development. An emotional response, something happening *within* buyers, characterizes the awesome connecting experience. David Lewis-Hodgson, director of Mindlab International, where they study the science of decisions, describes it this way: "Shopping experiences trigger brain activity that creates euphoric moments. These euphoric moments can be triggered by experiencing something unexpected."[10]

Connections are made emotionally, not logically. Experiences resonate and motivate when they touch people's hearts, not just their minds. The word *awesome* connotes an overwhelming feeling. B2B sellers need to engage at an emotional level with their buyers.

MEETING THE PREFERENCES OF TODAY'S BUYERS

Behaviorally, how can sellers create powerfully differentiating, awesome connecting experiences for their B2B buyers, who bring high expectations from their B2C experiences? CX researcher Esteban Kolsky concluded that 86 percent of buyers will pay more for an emotionally satisfying experience that is relevant and personalized than for something generic.[11] The value of a meaningful and unique experience significantly exceeds the value of the goods and services accompanying it.

The need for B2B sellers to catch up with consumer sales thinking is crystal clear. Less obvious is how B2B sellers can provide personalized experiences and help buyers to participate in creating what they want. Currently, sellers are not trained, equipped, or expected to:

- Cause an overwhelming feeling of admiration or respect.
- Provide the unexpected that triggers a euphoric response.
- Connect with buyers personally.
- Enable buyers to participate in creating what they want.
- Make buyers feel significant or important.

The value of a meaningful and unique experience significantly exceeds the value of the goods and service accompanying it.

These expectations seem less like a job description for sales and more like one for leadership. Buyers told us repeatedly that they want sellers to behave differently. Buyers resist "sales" behaviors and erect barriers to avoid sellers altogether. By contrast, they invite and welcome seller behaviors that produce awesome connecting experiences. Those behaviors are *leadership* behaviors.

Research Provides a Behavioral Blueprint

For over thirty years, Jim and Barry have continuously gathered and analyzed data about the behaviors of exemplary leaders.[12] By analyzing thousands of case studies and millions of survey responses from leaders around the globe and from all walks of life and backgrounds, they identified what leaders do when they are at their "personal best" as leaders. Their framework—The Five Practices of Exemplary Leadership®—has been adopted by scores of organizations for their leadership development programs, and hundreds of researchers have used the model in studies about the effectiveness of leaders across a variety of settings and circumstances.

The Five Practices of Exemplary Leadership® framework is an evidence-based operating system for leadership that's highly relevant for sellers. In our discussions and research with B2B buyers, we found that shifts in buyer demands directly corresponded to The Five Practices. Our research set out to determine just how buyers would respond to seller leadership, in the form of The Five Practices. Buyers in our studies spanned a variety of industries, company sizes, job functions, and ages. This cross-section of buyers represents different experience levels as B2B buyers, the number of sellers engaged with on a regular basis, the percentage of time spent working with sellers, and the buyer's actual role in the decision-making process, including whether purchasing decisions are made by the individual or by a group.

We surveyed 530 verified B2B buyers online over a four-month period. To measure The Five Practices, we used a slightly modified version of the *Leadership Practices Inventory*® (LPI), one of the most trusted and widely used leadership assessments available. It consists of thirty statements about leadership behaviors, each of which is assessed on a 10-point Likert frequency scale.[13] For each of the leadership behaviors we asked buyers:

> ➤ How frequently do sellers you choose to do business with exhibit this behavior?
> ➤ What would be the ideal frequency of this behavior in sellers you do business with?
> ➤ How likely would you be to meet with a seller who demonstrated this behavior?
> ➤ How likely would you be to buy from a seller who demonstrated this behavior?
> ➤ Which leadership behaviors are the most important?

In our research with sellers, we also invited them to share stories about their personal-best sales experiences.

Findings and Implications

The results of our research are eye-opening. Buyers definitely want sellers to stop selling and start leading:

> ➤ The ideal frequency of each leadership behavior is statistically higher (beyond a chance level of probability) than what buyers currently experience with the sellers they do business with.
> ➤ Buyers are significantly more likely to meet with sellers who exhibit these leadership behaviors.
> ➤ Buyers are substantially more likely to purchase from sellers who exhibit these leadership behaviors.

We now have a clear behavioral blueprint of what buyers want sellers to do.

THE FIVE PRACTICES OF EXEMPLARY LEADERSHIP®

Cam Johnson sells library automation and school security software. His company, COMPanion Corporation, dominates the field, a direct result of their commitment to customers. COMPanion continually pursues quality improvements to fulfill their mission of designing software with users in mind.

For Cam, opening the sale starts with researching the "mission, values, and beliefs" of the organization and learning all he can about the buyer. He looks for common ground and values, knowing this will give him a solid starting point.

Next, Cam asks open-ended discovery questions. When he does, he says, "I sit back and listen to every bit of information they give me." He wants to understand buyers' needs and long-term goals. When describing his personal best as a seller, Cam told us about a time when a buyer admitted he was seriously considering buying from one of Cam's competitors. Having established common ground and shared values, Cam knew what to do. He first thanked the buyer for sharing this information. Instead of bashing the competition, he then shared relevant data and industry insights. He continued to demonstrate his commitment to the buyer by asking how he could earn the opportunity to work together.

When the buyer eventually chose COMPanion, he told Cam it was because of that commitment to do whatever it would take to be a partner. Over time, Cam has continued to faithfully deliver on all the buyer's needs and affirm the buyer's decision.

For many sellers, this may sound like business as usual. On the surface, what Cam described is a classic consultative sale. Looking through the lens of leadership, though, something more is visible.

Cam, like many successful salespeople who are preferred by buyers, actually demonstrated The Five Practices of Exemplary Leadership:

- Model the Way
- Inspire a Shared Vision
- Challenge the Process
- Enable Others to Act
- Encourage the Heart

The Five Practices are all about behaviors. That makes them accessible to those who accept the challenge of leadership—the challenge of taking themselves, their buyers, and their organizations to new heights, of moving beyond the ordinary to the extraordinary. The Five Practices create the awesome connecting experience buyers crave.

In the remainder of this chapter, we introduce the five leadership practices and show how each is linked to buyer preferences. In Chapters Three through Twelve, you'll find stories from sellers who exemplify each leadership practice. Also provided are direct comments from buyers which further define and highlight the leadership behaviors they want sellers to exhibit more often.

The Five Practices create the awesome connecting experience buyers crave.

Model the Way

Model the Way is the leadership practice that addresses buyers' preferences for sellers who are consistent in displaying trustworthy behaviors.

To effectively *Model the Way*, you must first be clear about your own guiding principles. You must *clarify values by finding your voice.*

When you understand who you are and what your values are, you can give voice to those values in all you say and do.

As a seller/leader, your values aren't the only ones that matter. Everyone on the team—including your buyer—has principles that guide his or her actions. Therefore, you must *affirm the shared values* of the group. This requires involving everyone in establishing common values and holding everyone accountable for adhering to them. In this way, you will *set the example.* You will work to consistently align words and actions.

Model the Way matters because, without trust, there will be no sale. Buyers determine the trustworthiness of sellers by observing how they behave. Buyers are on the lookout for seller behaviors that demonstrate credibility, reliability, relate-ability, and an orientation focused mostly on the interests of others.

Inspire a Shared Vision

Inspire a Shared Vision is the leadership practice that will help you become more effective in designing and presenting the customized solutions that buyers prefer.

As a leader, you *envision the future by imagining exciting and ennobling possibilities.* To do so, you need a clear picture of the buyer's current circumstances and desired outcomes. A one-size-fits-all solution with generic features won't be exciting or ennobling. Translating those features into relevant benefits and a picture of each buyer's unique future will be.

Even so, you can't command the buyer's commitment; you have to inspire it. You must *enlist others in a common vision by appealing to shared aspirations.* Your vision will be exciting and ennobling when buyers can clearly see themselves as part of it.

It makes a difference when you Inspire a Shared Vision. This is how you gain buy-in before asking for the buy. It's how you deliver on buyer preferences for customization, and it's how you ignite buyers' passion for your solutions. Your buyers become, in essence, your internal sellers and leaders.

Challenge the Process

Challenge the Process is the leadership practice for creating unique and relevant value for your buyers, a daunting buyer preference and expectation.

Buyers are looking for sellers who can innovate and recognize opportunities by looking outside themselves and their usual resources for new and inventive solutions. You need to *search for opportunities by seizing the initiative and by looking outward for innovative ways to improve.*

Because innovation and change involve *experimenting and taking risks*, you can help buyers by creating a climate for experimentation, recognizing and supporting good ideas, and challenging business-as-usual thinking and systems. One way of dealing with the potential risks and failures of experimentation is *by constantly generating small wins and learning from experience.*

When you Challenge the Process, you create value. This makes a difference because buyers are disappointed when the experience isn't relevant, personal, and meaningful.

Enable Others to Act

Enable Others to Act is the leadership practice that positions your buyers to participate in creating precisely what they want.

Achieving success in sales, as in leadership, takes a collaborative team effort, one that springs from solid trust and enduring relationships. Leaders *foster collaboration by building trust and facilitating relationships.* At a time when there are increasing numbers of decision-makers involved in purchasing decisions,[14] you must find ways to engage every individual who will influence the decision and everyone who will be impacted by it, too.

To create true collaboration, you must *strengthen others by increasing self-determination and developing competence.* Your buyers and internal partners are more likely to give it their all when they feel trusted, informed, and empowered.

Of all the Practices, Enable Others to Act matters most to buyers. That's because buyers strongly prefer two-way dialogue and being directly involved in generating insights and making decisions.

Encourage the Heart

Encourage the Heart is the leadership practice that cements meaningful connections between you and your buyers.

Consider what you're asking buyers to do when they partner with you. Ushering in change is arduous for buyers, as they must convince others, take a risk with you, dedicate budget and other resources, and invest time in making all this happen. That's why it's important to *recognize contributions by showing appreciation for individual excellence.* Formally or informally, one on one or in group settings, in simple or grand gestures, you can keep your buyers feeling good about the work you're doing together so they'll continue to move it forward.

Being a leader requires showing appreciation for people's contributions and *celebrating the values and victories by creating a spirit of community.* This applies to your buyers and their extended teams, and to your internal team as well.

When you Encourage the Heart, you deliver on the buyer preference for meaningful connections with sellers. This makes a tremendous difference as you work to build buyer loyalty and meet your sales objectives.

◆ ◆ ◆

These five leadership practices—Model the Way, Inspire a Shared Vision, Challenge the Process, Enable Others to Act, and Encourage the Heart—are what people are doing when they are at their best as leaders, and there's abundant empirical evidence that these leadership practices matter. The more you use The Five Practices of Exemplary Leadership, the more you'll succeed with buyers by meeting their preferences.

IT'S TIME FOR REAL CHANGE

The case for change in seller behaviors is undeniable, not only from our research and experience, but in the work of many other academics and practitioners in the field. Despite all that's been researched and written, few sellers have significantly changed their behavior. While agreeing, in theory, that buyers want a connecting experience and value creation, sellers haven't sufficiently developed new skills to adapt to this new reality.

Perhaps there are misunderstandings about what gets results. Our seller-side research revealed an interesting disconnect. Seller stories about their personal bests include the leadership behaviors buyers desire, but sellers did not attribute their success to these behaviors. Instead, more than 75 percent of sellers' stories linked their success to persistence. But the word *persistence* isn't one buyers use in describing their preferences.

For sellers to make a change, they first need to understand what buyers want them to do. It's time to define behavioral changes in ways any seller can understand, observe, and adopt. Behaviorally, it's time for sellers to stop *selling* and start *leading*. The Five Practices of Exemplary Leadership is a behavioral blueprint for doing precisely that. It offers sellers a new paradigm, taking them in a fresh direction, while conforming to effective selling approaches described by practitioners and researchers.

2 | CREDIBILITY IS THE FOUNDATION OF BOTH LEADERSHIP AND MAKING THE SALE

ROBERT LEHRER HAS BEEN AN INDEPENDENT B2B group benefits broker for more than twenty years. He told us about an encounter with a cynical buyer. Right at the start, this buyer took exception to his ideas and repeatedly interrupted him. He tried to win her over with his charm and product benefits. She seemed uninterested in both. Robert knew he was at a disadvantage as a seller because, he believed, buyers inherently mistrust sellers and the clock was ticking, allowing little opportunity for him to demonstrate his trustworthiness.

After trying everything he knew to say or do, Robert gave up. It was long past the end of a typical day, and he was tired. In frustration, he candidly said, "I'm here only because you invited me to come and I'll be happy to leave if you'd like me to because I'd rather be home playing with our new pet rabbit right now."

What happened next took him by surprise.

The scowl on this woman's face suddenly turned into a look of curiosity, and she immediately asked me all about our new rabbit. She told me that she and her husband love rabbits. This led us to talk more about our personal interests, and eventually turned to why we were involved in our respective capacities, why what we did mattered, and how we could work with one another in a mutually beneficial fashion.

The outcome was one of the largest sales Robert had made to that point in his career. "A previous dud of an appointment," Robert said, "turned into a gem when we found common ground and had the chance to build mutual respect."

STEREOTYPICAL SALES BEHAVIORS DIMINISH SELLER CREDIBILITY

As Robert's experience shows, buyers too often assume the worst. They have their guard up and are reluctant to give sellers enough time to demonstrate trustworthiness. Pervasive negative stereotypes about sellers create a barrier to forming effective buyer/seller relationships. When a seller does get time with a buyer, there's no room for error. Buyers are skeptical and watching closely for any reason not to trust the seller.

For most sellers, this is an insult to their integrity and good intentions. It sets up a defensive posture and, depending on their personality, may lead them to be more forceful or more deferential when they call on buyers. They may respond in ways they wouldn't in non-selling situations. Desperation to reach buyers and rapidly prove oneself can backfire as sellers react to being negatively stereotyped, feeling mistrusted and unwelcome.

Inappropriate or unintentional reactions happen, for example, when quota-driven sellers make cold calls. In other conversations, most would never race through a script and ignore the initial response of the person they'd called. Yet sellers do this every day, showing disregard for buyers' time and interests, never mind their intelligence.

It happens, too, when appointment-setting sellers overpromise. In a single call, it's not uncommon to hear at least three promises: "I'll only take a few minutes of your time" and "We can fix your problem," followed by a promise of an appointment time. Buyers expect sellers to fulfill these promises by showing up on time, being brief and to the point, and offering a surefire solution. When sellers fail to make good on any of those promises, they've squandered an opportunity. As minor as these broken promises seem, they matter to buyers. At this early stage of the relationship, these assurances are all a buyer has to gauge the seller's credibility and trustworthiness.

Buyers seldom offer second chances once trust has been broken. "I refuse to do business with a liar or someone who breaks professional promises," one buyer told us.

CREDIBILITY MAKES A DIFFERENCE

In our buyer survey, we invited open-response comments to the question "What behaviors could a seller exhibit that would increase your likelihood of meeting with or buying from him or her?" More than one-third of the responses were related to the credibility of the seller.

To be credible simply means to be believable or to be worthy of being believed. What makes a seller—or anyone—worthy of being believed?

Communications experts refer to three "source credibility" characteristics. In assessing the source's believability—whether sellers, reporters, physicians, or priests; whether business managers, military officers, politicians, or civic leaders—researchers typically evaluate them on three criteria: their perceived *trustworthiness*, their *expertise*, and their *dynamism*. People who are rated more highly on these characteristics are considered by others to be more credible sources of information.[1]

Knowing about buyer perceptions and what buyers are evaluating helps sellers avoid inadvertent breaches of trust. Honesty is the number one factor in evaluating *trustworthiness*. As one buyer summed it up, the "most important aspect is honesty . . . keeping sales promises, even when things didn't go as they stated they would. I always continue to deal with people who keep promises."

Expertise is the second most important quality in determining credibility. People believe someone when they perceive that person knows what he or she is talking about. Expertise doesn't mean being "the" expert, nor does it require being smarter than everyone else or knowledgeable on every subject. It does mean that you should have deep knowledge about your product and service and the needs of your buyers. It also means that you are willing to acknowledge what isn't known and needs further investigation and analysis. As the seller, you know more about your product than buyers do, and presumably, buyers know more about their needs than you do.

> **Honesty is the number one factor in evaluating trustworthiness.**

Buyers want sellers to be experts in the products they sell; to have, as one buyer told us, "solid knowledge of the product." Buyers also expect sellers to be knowledgeable about the companies they represent and the industries they serve. But that's not all! B2B buyers depend on sellers to confer with them on matters requiring business acumen and an understanding of the buyer's business.

When a seller has expertise in all these areas, the relationship grows. The seller becomes a trusted advisor. Buyers describe the progression as starting with the seller "being able to demonstrate that they understand my business and how they can help from the first call" and developing into "exhibiting expert knowledge of whatever the product or solution involves." Over time, the relationship evolves into a connection characterized by mutual reliance and rapport. "There's a long-term seller I know who exhibits all of these," one buyer told us. "He positively affects the work we do; we almost consider him to a part of our own team."

In sales, trustworthiness and expertise sometimes take a back seat to *dynamism,* the third characteristic of source credibility, defined as great energy, force, or vigor. An energetic personality is one of the age-old stereotypes about selling. It's a characteristic many sales managers look for first and foremost when hiring sales people.

Dynamism may engage people, but it doesn't stand alone to demonstrate

> **Buyers, not unlike anyone else in life, will not believe the message if they don't believe in the messenger.**

credibility, and it can easily be overplayed. Buyers express a sense of fatigue and skepticism when it comes to sellers with big personalities, but little trustworthiness and expertise. All three are essential components of credibility.

In their survey responses, buyers explained that they want sellers to be "excited and eager about what you're selling without overselling it." They are looking for enthusiasm, but "not too enthusiastic." One buyer put it this way: "I want sellers to be personable and outgoing . . . and, mainly, when they come in to see me, that they've done their homework."

Sellers must take earning and sustaining credibility seriously. Buyers, not unlike anyone else in life, will not believe the message if they don't believe in the messenger. If they believe in you, they will be willing to listen to you and to buy into your message.

Credibility is the foundation for building a solid relationship between a buyer and seller. Likewise, credibility is the foundation of leadership.[2] Above all else, people must be able to believe in their leaders. To willingly follow someone, one must believe that the leader's words can be trusted, that the leader is personally passionate and enthusiastic about the work, and that the leader has the knowledge and the skill to deliver on promises made.[3]

Although not talking about sellers, the late John Gardner, former cabinet secretary and adviser to six U.S. presidents, offered a useful parallel when he said: "A loyal constituency is won when the people, consciously or unconsciously, judge the leader to be capable of solving their problems and meeting their needs."[4] As a seller/leader, before you can solve a problem or meet a need, you must first be judged capable of doing so. Credibility counts in selling in precisely the same ways it matters in leadership.

THE PRESCRIPTION FOR STRENGTHENING YOUR PERSONAL CREDIBILITY

Buyers are cynical. They question the trustworthiness and expertise of sellers, and they don't give sellers much of a chance to prove themselves. They may doubt sellers who display dynamism, assuming it's a quality that sellers overplay instead of showing trustworthiness and expertise. While not a cure-all for these unfortunate perceptions, sellers who focus on demonstrating and maintaining their credibility will differentiate themselves and gain buyer trust.

But how? What do sellers need to do to build and sustain credibility?

When it comes to credibility, the actions buyers look for in sellers precisely match what people say they look for in leaders they would willingly follow.[5] The *behavioral* evidence people look for when determining whether someone is credible boils down to one common refrain: "*They do what they say they will do*." Buyers used phrases like these to define credibility in action:

- ➤ "They deliver what they promise."
- ➤ "Talk is cheap. Following through is much more important."
- ➤ "Totally stands behind his statements."
- ➤ "Walks the walk" and "Talks the talk."
- ➤ "Held true to her word."

Not following through on commitments is a deal-breaker. Buyers do not tolerate poor follow-through. Many shared their disappointment in stories that ended the way one buyer described: "The salesperson didn't follow up on an order that was timely and lost our business." Some of those disappointments had lesser consequences for the buyer, but grave outcomes for the seller. For example, one buyer told us about a seller who said she would call on Monday morning but did not call until Monday afternoon. The buyer's response was to stop accepting calls from this seller: "If I can't trust her to call on time, what can I trust her with?"

Sellers may bristle at the harshness of this response. Being a few hours late, they reason, shouldn't be fatal to a relationship. What they're forgetting is how initially fragile that relationship between buyer and seller is. Until a seller has a chance to build trust, there is none. Breaking a small promise is a big deal when that's all the buyer has to gauge your credibility and trustworthiness.

Buyers reported a significant gap between the frequency of follow-through displayed by the sellers they choose to do business with and what they consider to be the ideal rate. What's more, of all the behaviors we asked buyers about, follow-through on promises and commitments ranked among the top three that matter most to buyers in their relationships with sellers. This is also the behavior that generated the greatest volume of most open-response comments in our surveys. Clearly, doing what you say you will do matters a great deal to your buyers.

As important as follow-through is for establishing credibility, it's also an essential ingredient in sustaining it. Buyers expect sellers to check in with them after the sale is made and the order is filled. Even satisfied buyers feel abandoned if sellers don't circle back to check on them.

At all stages of the sales process, the simple prescription for strengthening personal credibility is to "Do What You Say You Will Do" or DWYSYWD for short. Note that there are two parts to DWYSYWD: one is "say,"

> **Breaking a small promise is a big deal when that's all the buyer has to gauge credibility and trustworthiness.**

and the other is "do." Credibility is about the consistency between your words and actions. People listen to the words and pay attention to the actions. Then they measure the congruence. They hand down a judgment of "credible" when the two are aligned.

Buyers won't give you credit for your good intentions. All they can react to are your actions. But that doesn't mean you should merely act a certain way. On the contrary, aligning your words starts even deeper. It requires determining what you value.

MODEL THE WAY

The path to transition from being a traditional seller to becoming an exemplary leader is inward. The first step is getting in touch with your personal values and beliefs. Leaders must discover a set of principles, much like a compass, to guide their decisions and actions. In doing so, you find your voice and can speak with confidence about what matters to you. In fact, knowing who you are is essential in determining what to say yes to, and when to say no, in leading and in selling.

Yet leaders don't just speak for themselves. They also speak for their brand, their team, and their organization. Leadership is a dialogue, not a monologue. Therefore, you must reach out to others. You must understand and appreciate the values of your buyers and build a platform of shared values and aspirations. Exemplary sellers, like exemplary leaders, forge unity. They don't force it. They give people reasons to care beyond routine transactions or solutions to business needs.

Moreover, leaders deliver on their promises. You have to practice what you preach. Your actions must show others that you live by the values you profess. You must also ensure that others inside your organization adhere to the values that have been agreed to. It is this consistency between words and actions that builds your personal reputation and credibility.

When buyers observe sellers who Model the Way, they tell us how confident this makes them that sellers will deliver on promises and commitments made. These behaviors also increase buyers' beliefs that they are getting the best solution—the right product, right fit, at the right price.

As an exemplary seller, you engage in the leadership practice of Model the Way when you

- **Clarify values by finding your voice and affirming shared values.**
- **Set the example by aligning actions with shared values.**

3 | CLARIFY VALUES

AUDREY MORRISON SOLD CORPORATE HOUSING solutions to help companies relocate employees or host out-of-town executives and clients. She reached her annual quota by closing a nearly $400,000 deal with her very first client, a well-known company.

In discussing what led to her success, Audrey attributed it to something buyers rate much higher in importance than sellers typically do. She recognized the link between her core values and her actions. "I demonstrated great service," she said. "This is something that is very important to me in my day-to-day life. I think it's always important to be as helpful and friendly as possible." She conveys to buyers her authentic commitment to service, driven by her deeply held values, in a manner that gives them confidence in her.

Audrey also values authenticity and honesty. In closing her first deal, this meant being natural and being prepared to answer every question thoroughly and accurately, a practice she continues. "I'm not a pushy person," she told us. "I let my personality show and made it fairly casual, more like a conversation than a sales pitch. I wasn't overly aggressive just so I could close the deal."

> **There's a statistically significant relationship between the extent that sellers are clear about their leadership philosophy and both how proud they are to tell others where they work and how effective they report being in their jobs.**

The Personal-Best Sales Experience cases we've collected come directly from sellers like Audrey who made behavioral choices that resulted in sales success. Their choices were driven by internal beliefs. Before you can act on your beliefs and values, you must know what they are. To stand up for your beliefs, to have the courage of your convictions, and to align your actions with your words, you must first make a commitment to *Clarify Values*. As you work to become a leader, it's essential that you

- **Find your voice**
- **Affirm shared values**

Knowing your values means having guiding principles as you interact with buyers. What you say and do will reflect the "real you" and not a version of you that sets aside personal beliefs, standards, ethics, or ideals to do the work of selling. You have to say what you mean and mean what you say.

In addition to representing your authentic self, you also represent the beliefs and values of your organization and find common ground with each buyer, as well. Sellers, like leaders, aren't just speaking or acting for themselves. That's why you need to make sure there's agreement on a set of shared values between you, your organization, and your buyers. With that affirmation of common values, everyone can be held accountable to them.

FIND YOUR VOICE

Exemplary leaders are clear about their values, and that clarity gives them the courage to navigate difficult situations and make tough decisions. To become a credible leader—one buyers willingly choose to follow—you first must comprehend fully the values, standards, ethics, ideals, and deeply held beliefs that drive you. To be a credible leader *and* a respected seller, feeling proud of the work you do and the product or service you represent, you must connect what you believe with both what you say and what you do. You must find your own voice instead of parroting what others say, mimicking what others do, or pretending to be something you are not. Finding your voice begins with an inward journey to discover who you are. Then you need to genuinely express yourself and authentically communicate your beliefs in ways that uniquely represent who you are.

Jane Gentry, principal of Jane Gentry & Company, is clear about her values, which gives her a strong voice. She told us about how, when faced with an ethical dilemma, she chose to lose a sale instead of losing herself.

It all started with a referral from a fellow consultant. Jane and her partner were eager to work with the mid-market technology company in the south, and they spent hours poring over the specifics to be sure the price they proposed—in the mid six figures—was fair and profitable. This deal, they believed, was a sure thing, since there were no competitors in the running. At a time when the business needed a boost, this was a welcome referral and opportunity.

The night before the presentation, Jane received a call from the consultant who'd made the referral. Although he'd originally declined her offer to pay a referral fee that was in line with industry standards, he was now demanding that she mark the proposal up a whopping 30 percent for his cut of the deal. That would amount to tens of thousands just for making the introduction. When Jane told him "that number is unreasonable and, for all intents and purposes, it's outright stealing from the client," he became angry and screamed at her to "just do what I tell you!" Jane and her partner talked about the options.

It came down to this. I don't steal. I don't do things that are underhanded. I don't want any part of that. Maintaining my values, even when there's pressure or conflict, is what I will do every time because it's the right thing to do. Period. I don't want there to be a part of myself that I have to hide, that I don't want others to see. It takes energy to hide things, and my energy is better spent serving people, not stealing from them. If I had agreed to do this, I'd never be able to look that client in the eye or hold my head high.

For Jane, and for all exemplary leaders, values are non-negotiable. Despite all the work they'd already done, she and her partner decided to bow out of the presentation. Despite the need for a big new account, what they wanted most was to maintain their principles. Walking away was the only way they could do that.

Sellers, especially those who are new to the profession, may not realize how important it is to bring themselves—complete with values intact—authentically into their work. Many mistakenly set aside "who they are" in the hope that they can "sell anything to anyone." They think this is what's expected of them and will bend their principles when they feel that's what it takes to make a sale. It's precisely this incongruity that causes buyer mistrust and diminishes the dignity of the sales profession.

Exemplary sellers are not thespians, acting on some grand stage. Instead of putting on an act to sell, when you find your voice, you will behave in accord with your values. Your values will become your internal compass and guide your actions. This is how you'll know when to say "yes" and when to say "no" because your compass will keep you on course and in alignment with what matters most to you. When your values become your personal bottom line, absolute and unshakeable like Jane's are, you will not be tempted to shift or compromise to suit the situation. Instead, being clear about your values will make you more consistent.

With values clarity, you'll also become more confident. By finding your voice and reconciling your actions, words, and core beliefs, you will be interacting with buyers in ways that display inner confidence. It's the self-assurance that's necessary to express ideas, stay the course, make decisions, act with determination, and take charge of your life instead of impersonating others who may be held up as "best" or "top" sellers.

Your credibility and sales effectiveness will soar as buyers both sense and see evidence of your confidence, consistency, and congruency. They will respond to you as a leader instead of resisting you as a seller. They will trust you.

On the other hand, if you lack values clarity, buyers will see inconsistencies that cause them to doubt or mistrust you. This happens most often in the "moments of truth" every seller faces. Here are five classic situations that trip up sellers who have not spent time discovering and dedicating themselves to their own personal values:

> **Your values are your internal compass and guide your actions. This is how you'll know when to say "yes" and when to say "no."**

☑ Little White Lies.

Sellers tell "little white lies" to save face. It happens when they skip or reschedule appointments, miss deadlines, or fail to deliver on promises. In our research, "honesty" is the word used most frequently when buyers are asked what they want from sellers. Honesty is also the characteristic of admired leaders that's selected most frequently in surveys that have involved over 100,000 people around the globe.[1]

☑ No Price Integrity.

Many sellers don't maintain price integrity or contract terms when yielding will help them close a deal. Buyers know that month-end and year-end deals are common sales tactics. They delay decisions in anticipation of more favorable terms. When price concessions materialize, buyers wonder how much lower the price could go and why sellers first tried suckering them into a higher price.

☑ Divulging Confidential Information.

Sellers divulge confidential information about a buyer's competitors to create a sense of urgency, to capitalize on the fear of missing out, or to demonstrate the popularity of their product. Buyers may be pleased to learn something about their competitors. Nevertheless, they're unsettled by realizing sellers could also be sharing confidential information about them.

☑ No Accountability.

Sellers don't take responsibility for errors or misunderstandings. When buyers are dissatisfied, they don't care who made the mistake. They don't want to be blamed or met with a defensive reaction. They want sellers to follow through, to make it right, and to deliver what was promised.

☑ Self-Serving Choices.

Sometimes, sellers make choices that negatively impact buyers. Examples include upselling an unnecessary feature to earn additional incentive pay, delaying an order so the revenue counts in a later quota period, or reallocating resources from an established customer to win over a new prospect. Buyers notice and feel trust has been breached when sellers make choices like these.

After clarifying your values and finding your voice, you'll discover situations like these will be easier to navigate. Even so, be on the lookout for old habits or external factors that can take you off course. Remember, buyers are always watching to see what you'll do. Being a credible leader—someone buyers will choose to follow—means you must consistently live your values. You have to put into action what you stand for and be the example for others to follow.

AFFIRM SHARED VALUES

Finding your voice is essential to building commitment to your organization and the buyer. But for leaders, clarifying values does not stop there. You also represent others' voices and values as a seller, and you must discern the fit with those beliefs without compromising your own. You must affirm the ideals you share with the company or brand you represent. As a seller, you must simultaneously represent the interests of your buyer by following through on the commitments you've made. That's not always easy to do.

Perhaps you've been in a quandary like the one Patrick Fariss faced as a K-12 education sales representative for Texas Instruments. Patrick could've taken the easy way out. Instead, acting on his belief that buyers should feel valued and respected, he decided to deliver a tough message personally.

What happened was that Patrick's company was ending support for a product in which a Houston-area school district had invested heavily. The district, said Patrick, "had no desire (or funding) to transition to our newest model, which would cost the district upwards of a million dollars. When I found out that we would discontinue support of this product, I realized that we needed to get in front of the customer as quickly as possible. We needed to make sure they had all the information and did not hear this before the official announcement." This was a brave choice, driven by Patrick's values.

We knew it would not be a pleasant meeting. Seeing the need to get in front of this, I brought my manager in, and we scheduled a meeting with the key contacts. In the meeting, we talked about how we valued their investment and wanted to provide support as they planned ahead for the coming two to three years. We shared the information and then sat quietly as they let us have it. They were frustrated and voiced regret over their investment in our product. There was little we could say or do, but we wanted to let our customer have their voices heard. As the face of the company, it's our responsibility to be there in the good and the bad. We left that tense meeting beaten up, but knowing we had done the right thing.

For many sellers, that would have been the end of the engagement. Duck-and-cover may be the easy way, but it wasn't Patrick's way. He was committed to his own and his company's ideals to do right by every customer.

> *We followed up and reassured them that we wanted to help them transition in any way we could. A few weeks later, once the dust had settled, I received a call from the customer asking for another meeting where we could begin to plan for the purchase of our latest technology. They appreciated our being up-front, and we ended up with orders of $1 million over the next two years.*

Win, lose, or draw, Patrick could feel proud of the work he did with this buyer. He was true to himself and did what was right for both his company and his buyer. He was also personally committed to the values of the brand he represented and the buyers he served. This helped him sustain his credibility in an uncomfortable situation. Despite the company's decision to change its offering, Patrick took responsibility for delivering the message and finding a remedy. "Doing the right thing for your customer might not always be easy," concludes Patrick, "but if you're willing to take the heat, you have a better chance at winning long term."

Sellers are usually the face of their companies with buyers. What the seller promises is what the buyer expects. When sellers misrepresent or overstate what the company can deliver, buyers mistrust both the seller and the company. Similarly, buyers expect sellers to deliver on brand promises they've seen in marketing messages or marketplace positioning. The seller and sales organization must be aligned to avoid mixed messages and disappointed buyers.

If you lack shared ideals or ignore them, buyers will see inconsistencies that cause them to doubt you.

This burden falls primarily on sellers. Sellers are responsible for checking, setting, and managing buyers' expectations. Sellers are responsible for knowing internal systems, deadlines, and capabilities and correctly communicating these to buyers. When exceptions are needed, it's a seller's obligation to check with internal partners first rather than making unrealistic promises to buyers. When changes, disruptions, unforeseen circumstances, or problems arise, it's also the seller's duty to be proactive in alerting buyers.

In other words, buyers see sellers as the leaders of their internal teams. They look to sellers as they would look to leaders, fully expecting them to mobilize people and resources to make things happen. Sellers can only do this if they have affirmed shared ideals throughout the organization.

Often, shared ideals are already in place. Sellers simply access, magnify, or operationalize them. If your company has a strong value of "delivering on time every time," this is the shared ideal you and your internal partners must work together to meet. But if the company's primary value is to produce "only the finest," then you need to align with this shared ideal. Demanding expedited delivery that compromises quality would not be an appropriate action.

If you lack shared ideals or ignore them, buyers will see inconsistencies that cause them to doubt you. This happens most often in "moments of truth" every seller faces. Here are five examples of times when sellers deviate from shared ideals and brand promises:

> **Shared values are important in every partnership.**

☑ **Sellers Are Cold Calling.**

Quantity over quality leads to unprofessional voice and email messages. Seller expectations of being rebuffed by buyers cause them to deliver a rushed monologue. Lack of pre-call planning makes most cold contacts generic and uninteresting.

☑ **Buyers Are Disgruntled.**

Defensiveness or pass-along blame only fuel buyer ire. The more a seller resists hearing and understanding a buyer's objections, the worse it gets. Sellers must act as ambassadors to represent real or implied promises made by the company.

☑ Sellers Prefer a "Lone Wolf" Approach.

Or the seller may adopt an us/them mentality. They position themselves as being on the buyer's side and flaunt their disregard for the company's protocols. While buyers might appreciate the favors or exceptions they receive, they also lose respect for the disloyal seller and the sales organization.

☑ Sellers Are Surly.

Or they may be abrupt, overly casual, impolite, rushed, or lacking confidence. Buyers want sellers who call on them to be friendly, personable, professional, positive, polite, and confident. Attitude is an expression of ideals.

☑ Sellers Express a Lack of Confidence.

This may plant seeds of doubt in buyers' minds, and buyers then lack confidence in the seller's company's products, services, or standards. Buyers look to sellers to present prices and solutions with the utmost of confidence.

In these instances, and others like them, sellers give buyers reasons to wonder about the credibility of both the seller and his or her sales organization. If a seller is not consistent in affirming shared ideals, the buyer's perception will be that something is amiss.

When clear shared ideals have not been established, the burden still falls to the seller. In this case, the seller—as would any leader—works to understand the values of others and to create alignment everyone can support. Leaders build on agreement. They know that shared values are foundational pillars for building productive and genuine working relationships. That's why you must also align for shared values with your buyers.

Shared values are important in every partnership. Sellers who build trust- and values-based partnerships with their buyers have a distinct advantage. Charles Green, founder and CEO of Trusted Advisor Associates, illustrates how the sales process is a powerful (but missed!) opportunity to create trust-based partnerships.[2] He explains that most corporate sales training programs focus on providing a buying motivation through the product's features and ability to solve a problem. Some, Charlie says, go further by teaching sellers to position themselves as good business partners, adding value as consultants. Few, however, get to the level of trust that buyers respond to personally, and powerfully. This deeper level of partnership is impossible without trust. Shared values are fundamental to strong, trusting bonds.

Finding shared values with your buyer doesn't mean abdicating your own values. It also doesn't mean asking buyers to adopt your values. Sellers won't change buyers' minds or hearts when it comes to values. Values are deeply personal and meaningful. It would be an affront to suggest a buyer choose different values or to ignore the buyer's core values. Shared values build on personal values. You can't find common ground unless you first have solid grounding in your own values. What you're looking for is the natural overlap between your values and your buyer's values. That commonality is the starting place for building consensus.

Getting there requires discovery and dialogue. Open discussion about what matters to people is engaging, refreshing, and differentiating. This will be a process, not a pronouncement. As you gain agreement on shared values, you'll also be gaining commitment to a partnership. That's why leaders must hold themselves and others accountable to the set of values they share.

Take Action: Clarify Values

To Clarify Values, begin *by finding your voice and affirming shared values.* These are your values for all your life, professional and personal. Your values and voice won't waver when you're in a selling situation. This means you must:

1. Identify the values you use to guide the choices and decisions you make.

2. Find your own authentic way of talking about what's important to you.

3. Help your buyers and internal partners to articulate why they do what they do and what they care about.

4. Build consensus with your buyer around values, principles, and standards.

5. Make sure people adhere to agreed-on values and standards before, during, and after a purchase has been made.

4 | SET THE EXAMPLE

DAN OLEXA IS A COACHING ENTREPRENEUR AND FORMER
seller who believes in maintaining long-term relationships with buyers
and takes personal risks to stand up for this value. He considers these
moments to be among his personal bests as a seller.

> *I'm not about turning a quick sale and running to the next prospect. I
> like to build long-term relationships with my clients. Over the course
> of my career, I've run afoul of some employers because I focused on
> the long-term profitability of a client rather than making the most
> dollars on every single job. I stood up for my clients at the risk of my
> employment status. I pushed back on irrational and unfair charges,
> shoddy work, and unacceptable excuses. My clients rewarded these
> behaviors with increasing sales volume, and I become the "go-to"
> person for answers, ideas, and jobs that were problems for my
> competitors.*

Leaders like Dan know buyers don't want to do business with sellers who are in it for the quick sale and then are gone, never to be seen again. What's more, they understand that a commitment to long-lasting relationships means working with internal partners to deliver on promises. Dan, for example, told us how his production team recognizes his passion and does their part to make Dan's relationships work:

"While at times they didn't like being pressed to work harder or be more attentive, they understood that I held myself to the same standards. I approach them as a co-worker, looking for and helping to provide solutions, rather than pointing out problems and walking away."

It would, undoubtedly, have been easier for Dan to back down. He might have earned higher commissions if he'd spent more time prospecting new business and less time championing his customers' causes inside his organization. He could have rationalized his values away by saying buyers aren't loyal, his boss was making demands on him to move on to the next buyer, or the quality issues weren't his responsibility. Instead, Dan demonstrated a fierce commitment to his buyers.

> **Those sellers who feel most proud of what they do and most effective in their jobs are those who report most frequently setting a personal example of what they expect of others.**

Buyers don't see behaviors like Dan's often enough. It's why so many of them echoed the yearning for sellers, as one buyer put it, to be "sincere and personable with their approach and conversation instead of just being about making money." It's why it's a novelty for them to find sellers who "show dedication to do what's best." And it's why another buyer told us he's been looking for more than twenty years to find "a seller with principles who stands up for the customer and only sells products that are ethical."

Most buyers have encountered sellers who play fast and loose with the truth. Stereotypes abound, as do terms like huckster, peddler, snake oil salesman, haggler, and cutthroat negotiator. Sellers may perpetuate these low expectations. Most are under pressure—real, perceived, or self-imposed—to reach sales quotas. Surrounded by others who do whatever it takes to make a sale, many sellers abandon customer-centric practices and opt to serve their own interests instead.

That's hardly the kind of commitment buyers want to see. They much prefer the commitment demonstrated by sellers like Dan. Here's the good news. The data clearly show that you have a powerful opportunity to differentiate yourself with buyers by demonstrating a sincere commitment to them and a high set of ethical standards. For example, sellers in the top third of the distribution on the Model the Way leadership behaviors are a whopping 69 percent more likely to agree that they're effective in meeting the demands of their work than those in the bottom third of the distribution, and they report being more than 31 percent more effective than those in the middle of this distribution. You are off to a great start when you clarify your values, find your voice, and affirm shared values. The next step in your leadership journey is to *Set the Example*. To do this, it's essential to:

- **Live the shared values**
- **Teach others to model the values**

In practicing these essentials, you become an example to your internal partners and your buyers. You represent what your company stands for and create a climate in which everyone involved commits to aligning themselves with shared values.

LIVE THE SHARED VALUES

Joey Nanai, a regional sales executive with New Zealand's Concur Technologies, was ready when opportunity knocked. He gave an elevator pitch (in an actual elevator!) to a CEO at a networking event. The CEO was impressed and invited him to meet with the company's finance director. Before the meeting, Joey researched the company to understand their values, vision, and mission. He incorporated this information into his presentation, authentically representing his own values, too. When he later asked for feedback about why they gave him the sale, they told him it was because he showed genuine interest in

Buyers commit to sellers who commit to them.

finding ways to help their business grow and achieve their vision. Because of the values he shared, they trusted Joey to give them the support they would need going forward.

Joey did not modify or misrepresent his own values. Nor did he expect his buyer to change a thing about their values, vision, or mission. Joey found natural alignment and built the connection from that point of overlap. He spent time learning about the buyer and put thought into what they'd need and how he, uniquely, could support them. Joey's actions revealed his commitment.

Buyers commit to sellers who commit to them. One buyer raved about what he called "a best-in-class seller who is always concerned that I'm receiving the best service possible. She is committed to her job, and that just makes me want to partner more by buying from her company more because she is showing that they are committed to making me successful."

Without a seller's commitment, buyers look elsewhere. In fact, buyers boycott entire brands if they don't perceive corporate commitment to aligning with their needs and interests or to the causes they believe in. Empowered buyers vote with their wallets.

Buyers want you to care about the things that matter to them. They want you to demonstrate your commitment in visible ways. They want you to *live the shared values* of your brand promise. They want your personal commitment to them. When sellers reveal a lack of commitment to customers, buyers unite to demand change. When United Airlines dragged a passenger off a plane, the result was a loss of credibility about being "the friendly skies" and significantly raised the compensation for passengers who are bumped from flights. Buyer reactions to Uber's surge pricing and seeming lack of concern for passenger safety cost the company dearly and slowed their growth.

 More than two-thirds of buyers felt that sellers were credible and trustworthy in direct proportion to how frequently they modeled the way.

Your commitment to each buyer must be clear and consistent. When it comes to shared values, buyers try to describe what they need with comments like these:

> **Buyers are human. Humans respond to emotional connection. Emotional connections come from spending time with people.**

➤ "I go with an instinctual feeling about sellers' character based on their demeanor. If I feel they are being pushy or pressuring me for self-serving purposes, that has a very negative impact."

➤ "Sellers must be passionate, personal, creative, ambitious, honest, trustworthy, timely, and dedicated to customers."

➤ "The main thing is positivity. If they're negative or act like they don't want to waste their time doing business, I won't buy from them."

Leaders demonstrate commitment by spending time with their buyers and internal partners, by choosing language that reinforces shared values, by asking purposeful questions that focus on the shared values, and by seeking feedback.

Buyers are human. Humans respond to emotional connection. Emotional connections come from spending time with people. Having superior skills and tools may appeal to a buyer's logic, but emotion is what opens and sustains relationships. Spending time with buyers gives you greater opportunity to form connections, prove your commitment, and display shared values through your actions. Similarly, you need to spend sufficient time with internal partners so that they know you and connect with you.

How you spend your time is the single clearest indicator of what's important to you. Spending more time with the people you rely on and on the values that matter is essential to bolstering credibility, demonstrating commitment, and building consensus.

In the time you spend with your buyers and partners, pay close attention to the topics and language you choose. Think about the subtext of words and phrases commonly used to describe the work sellers do: hunting, farming, going in for the kill, bagging a prospect, circling the wagons, winning, overcoming, running plays, full court press, flip, grind, land, spear. . . . This lexicon of aggressive-sounding phrases can trap you into thinking negatively about your buyers or in a win-lose relationship with them.

Exemplary leaders understand the power of words and use them with care. Your words give voice to your beliefs and convey your expectations about how others are to behave. If your internal partners hear you referring to buyers with derogatory terms like chiseler, sucker, grape, grinder, slide ruler, gatekeeper, or tire kicker, you're inadvertently signaling that they, too, can show disdain for the buyer. You can't ask someone to give his or her best for a buyer you're disparaging, even if your use of these terms is not intended to be offensive.

> **When you ask questions, you create a path for buyers to follow and lead them to new places.**

The words you choose have an effect on how others see you, too. If you refer to yourself as a closer, you may raise suspicions about your values. Calling yourself a sales machine puts emphasis on what you produce, not on who you work with or how you conduct yourself. If the terms you use suggest superiority, imagine how your internal partners might feel.

What you say matters. How you say it matters, too. Be sure your shared values are reflected by your language. Words help build a frame around people's view of the world. Frames provide the context for partnerships and influence how people interpret events and intentions. The words partner, teammate, and colleague put a collaborative frame around how you work with others.

Leaders' frames include others in the picture. Connections count. Richardson's 2016 Selling Challenges Study revealed that the top three challenges for sellers result from shifts in buyer behavior that make it very difficult to identify, qualify, and connect with prospects. To get through, they claim that sellers must be "skilled in conducting a valuable and valued needs dialogue with buyers when the opportunity arises. At the same time, they must be able to provide meaningful insights during their brief encounters. . . . They also must have the will, skill, and tools to be deeply prepared and understand their prospect's business."[1]

To understand your buyer's business, ask purposeful questions. When you ask questions, you create a path for buyers to follow and lead them to new places. The questions you ask also let people know what is top of mind for you. Asking, for example, "What are you hoping to accomplish?" indicates your interest in understanding your buyer's needs, whereas asking "What's your budget?" signals that a recommendation will be based on the investment level. Both are legitimate questions when asked at the right time, but they indicate different priorities. Questions help keep everyone—including you—on the right track.

Deb's extensive research with buyers found that buyers believe purposeful questions demonstrate seller commitment and care. Sellers who used eight types of purposeful questions they learned in workshops were described by buyers as understanding, trusted, smart, insightful, knowledgeable, and partners. By asking purposeful questions, sellers aligned themselves with buyer values and set the example for openness and sharing in the buyer/seller relationship. Sellers and buyers alike in this study reported greater success, stronger relationships, and deeper commitment to each other.[2]

Your buyers and internal partners want an invitation to express their preferences and needs. If you don't ask, they may not tell you what you could be doing differently. If you don't ask and set the example for receiving feedback graciously, you'll have a harder time getting others to accept your feedback. Sharing values isn't a one-time exercise. It's an ongoing commitment that is measured by your actions. Better to give and receive feedback than to let that commitment fizzle due to discomfort with feedback.

The pinnacle of commitment that sellers can demonstrate to buyers is a personal investment in aligning with them by living shared values.

By living shared values, sellers reach the pinnacle of commitment. They do what all exemplary leaders do—align their actions to a common set of principles and beliefs. This kind of engagement goes deeper than service, availability, and meeting business needs. It goes to the core of the person.

TEACH OTHERS TO MODEL THE VALUES

As a leader, you aren't the only one who must be setting the example. Ideally, shared values will create mutual accountabilities and reciprocal role modeling. Your role is to make sure that you, your internal partners, and your buyers are all keeping the promises you've made to each other and are staying true to your shared values. Look for opportunities to provide a good example and discover ways to teach and coach others the way Dan did to shift his company's thinking about customer satisfaction.

You create opportunities when you ask for and accept feedback because that makes it easier for others to hear your feedback. Buyers respond favorably to this kind of humility and commitment. One told us, "I typically buy from a seller who both asks for feedback and gets genuinely excited about my accomplishments, which resulted from his recommendations. This makes me feel like my success is important to him, and I'm not just a customer."

In sales functions, it's a best practice to conduct post-mortem assessments of sales meetings and presentations. Include in that after-action review a question to find out, directly from buyers, what seller actions influenced their decisions. Soliciting that feedback will help to boost sales results. The answers to your question will yield valuable insights into how your actions impact buyers. Improvement isn't possible until you understand the cause-and-effect relationship between your actions and buyer decisions. While sales coaches may observe and offer similar feedback, there's no substitute for the direct feedback and perspective of the buyer. Additionally, obtaining buyer feedback shows your commitment and earns the buyer's respect.

Leaders periodically ask for 360-degree feedback. They want to know how they are being viewed by and how they are impacting their various constituent groups. It's an exercise in vulnerability, one that requires true commitment. Leaders know they're setting an example when they ask for feedback, graciously accept it, and work to make changes based on it.

Critical incidents present opportunities to teach your internal partners and buyers important lessons about how to respond in accord with shared values.

What would happen if you asked your buyers for feedback? What level of commitment would that demonstrate to them? How might it give you even more opportunities to align your shared values and set an example for them? In our research with buyers, they eagerly shared their thoughts about sellers (good and bad!). They seem to appreciate the opportunity to be heard. So why not give them a chance to share their feedback directly with you?

Remember, B2B buyers are being conditioned by their B2C experiences. In B2C, buyers are continually invited to offer feedback. They receive emails every time they seek help-desk support, check out of a hotel, or complete a flight. Many major retailers print survey invitations right on register receipts. In B2C, buyers offer feedback, even when it's not solicited. Posting social media reviews has become the new norm. Since buyers are so accustomed to giving feedback, perhaps an outlet for doing so with you would be particularly welcome. It would demonstrate, in one more way, your level of commitment to the buyer.

Buyer research conducted for *DISCOVER Questions® Get You Connected* revealed an easy way to do this. It's a simple service check using an I (Issue) Question.[3] The question to ask is: "What can I be doing differently to better support you?" It's a proactive question that demonstrates commitment and invites feedback that preserves relationships.

Another way to show others what you expect and hold them accountable is to confront critical incidents. These are the unexpected, chance occurrences that test every leader while also providing fertile ground for learning. Critical incidents present opportunities for you to teach your internal partners and buyers important lessons about how to respond in accord with shared values.

Of course, doing so isn't always easy. David Richman, a business broker from Connecticut, had to make certain everyone involved in the closing of a sale adhered to the principles and standards they'd agreed on. It was contentious; attorneys representing both sides did not get along. The attorneys were so enmeshed in personal conflict that the deal was at risk of not closing. Here's what David said he did:

> *I brought each attorney into an office separately and read each the riot act in private, and then went on to tell them this might be the last transaction they ever do if I have anything to say about it. I reminded them of their fiduciary responsibility, their pledge to protect their clients, and the fact that I have now been sitting in a room for close to five hours and I'm prepared to sit for another eight hours if they are. I then spoke with the buyer and*

Through stories, leaders pass on lessons about shared values, define culture, and get others to work together.

seller (whom I am representing) and let them both know we might
be here for a while.

Within ten minutes the funds were wired to the account. The next
day I had four emails from those who were in the room thanking me
for keeping the deal together and standing up to the attorneys!

Critical incidents become teaching moments. Leaders use them to teach others and for their own learning. Just as we've found for leaders, the most successful sellers are the best learners.[4] Learning is a master skill. Continuous learning is yet another way for you to demonstrate competence and build credibility while showing your commitment to your buyers. As we'll explore more in Chapters Seven and Eight, leaders actively seek learning opportunities.

One more way you can teach others to model the shared values is by telling stories. Stories are a powerful tool for teaching people about what's important and what's not, what works and what doesn't, what is and what could be.[5] Through stories, leaders pass on lessons about shared values, define culture, and get others to work together.

Vernon Hills is a gifted storyteller. He's spent most of his career as a fundraiser for nonprofit organizations. He speaks to potential donors one-to-one and, sometimes, in group settings. He told us a story about presenting to a Rotary club when he talked about shared values. Like Rotarians, Vernon works to make a difference in his community.

People know I'm passionate about helping people and being a voice for
the voiceless. I have the privilege to represent the underdogs from all
walks of life and to tell their stories of hope and restoration. On that
particular day, I told a story about a young mother who left an abusive
relationship. She was living in her car with her two children, parking
in motel parking lots each night. She had no money, and her children
were extremely hungry. She was feeding them ice from the ice machine
just so they could have the sensation of crunching on something.

After Vernon told this riveting story, including the happy ending about how his organization helped the family, the room was silent, awash with emotion. The next day, Vernon received a call. The Rotary club wanted to make a donation. Vernon's story struck a chord because it was one many successful businesspeople could relate to. They knew first-hand what it was like for those children and wanted more mothers and their children to be helped.

Vernon used a powerful story to prompt action that aligned with shared values. He taught his audience how to do the work that expressed their values. Vernon also uses this story to teach others how to do the work of fundraising. He knows that stories are remembered and repeated. They have a multiplying effect in setting examples over and over again.

As a leader, you send signals about how others are to act. Putting thought into the signals you send will make you more effective. Setting the right example will produce more of the right results. Invest time with your buyers and internal partners and make wise choices in the language you use and the questions you ask. Invite feedback. Teach by leveraging critical incidents and telling stories. This is how you will stop selling and start leading.

Take Action: Set the Example

To Set the Example, align actions with shared values. This requires that you:

1. Keep your commitments and consistently follow through on your promises.

2. Spend your time in ways that reflect what you say is important.

3. Ask purposeful questions that keep buyers and team members focused on the values and priorities that are most essential.

4. Routinely ask for feedback from buyers and others about how your actions affect them.

5. Make adjustments based on feedback you receive so that you maintain alignment and effectiveness with buyers and internal partners.

INSPIRE A SHARED VISION

As a seller, you are a purveyor of hope for the future. Buyers turn to you for solutions. As an exemplary seller, you attract buyers and make sales by painting the picture of a brighter tomorrow, showing what's possible when everyone works together for a common purpose.

But one person's vision, no matter how exciting, won't make an extraordinary difference. It's not enough that you believe some action would be beneficial for your buyer. If you alone see, understand, and believe in your vision, it won't generate the organized movement necessary to activate it. You need others—including buyers—to see and believe in the exciting future possibilities. Leaders breathe life into visions. They communicate hopes and dreams so others can clearly understand and share them as their own. They show others how the long-term vision of the future serves their values and interests.

The vision of the future portrayed by some sellers is fabricated, exaggerated, or farfetched, filled with "blue sky" promises. Buyers react negatively when sellers over-promise and under-deliver. Unfortunately, this happens often enough that buyers are suspicious when they hear a seller's vision. They want to see themselves in it, but aren't sure they can believe the possibilities being described. That's why credibility is vitally important to leadership and accomplishing extraordinary sales.

To Inspire a Shared Vision is to fully understand what buyers want to see and experience when they reach the future they envision. Moreover, they want to be involved in crafting the vision for their future state. By aligning with the buyer's unique vision and values, sellers are more effective and better able to appeal to shared aspirations.

As an exemplary seller, you engage in the leadership practice of Inspire a Shared Vision when you

- **Envision the future by imagining exciting and ennobling possibilities.**
- **Enlist others in a common vision by appealing to shared aspirations.**

5 | ENVISION THE FUTURE

THE DESIGNERS CONSIDERED THE PRESENTATION A HUGE success. Their buyers, Minnie and Stewart, said it was "amazing" and "everything looked so good." They loved the floor plans, furniture, fabric choices, and window treatments. But Judith Cervone, interior design sales project manager, was concerned. If everyone was so pleased with this redecorating project for a penthouse in a New York City highrise, what was keeping the contract from being signed and moving forward?

It was Judith's job to close top-dollar projects, and this was one of them. Her role included pairing designers with buyers and working in the background to coordinate details and make sure buyers were pleased. Judith decided to probe and find out why Minnie and Stewart hadn't committed. After all, they'd told Judith this would be their dream home for retirement, and they'd seemed eager to begin.

Following the presentation in the retail design center on Saturday, Minnie and Stewart spent the rest of the weekend discussing it and trying to remember all they'd seen and heard. They felt overwhelmed when Judith connected with them on Monday. She set up a time to meet in their home, where there would be no distractions and the samples could be displayed on-site to bring the vision to life.

Judith packed presentation boards, samples, sketches, and designs, along with a step-by-step plan for delivery and installation. This time, it was easier for Minnie and Stewart to imagine the renovation as Judith helped them envision their retirement, room by room. When she and her design team finished, Stewart wrote a check for the full amount, no hesitation and no questions asked.

What was the difference between the first presentation and the second one? Judith's ability to envision the future and imagine the possibilities of the proposed design, one that she also made Minnie and Stewart see as well.

 Sellers who shape their buyer's vision ultimately close more sales. The data shows that the more sellers report that they describe a compelling image of what our future could look like they also indicate not only being clearer about what's expected of them, but more productive in their jobs.

Exemplary leaders are forward-looking, which is a quality that buyers expect in sellers. They envision the future and see greater opportunities to come. They imagine that extraordinary feats are possible and that something special can emerge from the ordinary. They develop a vision that is an ideal and unique image of the future for the common good.

This vision doesn't belong to the leader alone. It must be a shared vision. Everyone has hopes, dreams, and aspirations. Everyone wants tomorrow to be better than today. Shared visions attract more people, sustain higher levels of motivation, and withstand more challenges than those held by only a few. You need to make sure that what you can see is also something others can see. That's what Judith did for Minnie and Stewart.

To *Envision the Future*, you must master these two essentials:

- **Imagine the possibilities**
- **Find a common purpose**

You begin with the end in mind by imagining what might be possible. Finding a common purpose inspires both sellers and buyers to do whatever it takes to make the vision a reality.

In our research, there was a wide gap between buyers and sellers on the importance of Inspire a Shared Vision. Sellers consistently chose it as the practice they believe is most important to buyers. However, buyers felt it was the least important leadership practice. This is an intriguing discovery because Jim and Barry have found, in more than three decades of research, that being forward-looking is the quality that most differentiates leaders from individual contributors. What might explain why buyers don't value Inspire a Shared Vision as much as the empirical research on leadership suggests?

Comments from buyers reveal the underlying problem. Buyers don't take a seller's vision seriously when the seller hasn't yet demonstrated credibility. Buyers doubt the vision will ever come true. They are jaded and think these are just words or jargon used to make a sale. Since they don't yet believe the messenger, they can't believe the message. As one buyer said, "Before anything can move forward, I need to know that the seller has my best interests as his or her best interests." Without a foundation of credibility and trustworthiness, few buyers will be interested in your vision, even when it would otherwise be compelling.

Once sellers build a solid foundation of credibility, they can then Inspire a Shared Vision that reflects imagination and a deep understanding of others' hopes, dreams, and aspirations.

IMAGINE THE POSSIBILITIES

When Brian Snider started selling newspaper advertising, he was assigned the local restaurant category. Being the newest person, he was working the last week of the year, when the office was nearly empty and reaching prospects was highly unlikely. Brian decided to spend that week indulging in possibility thinking.

Leaders turn possibilities into opportunities. They imagine that extraordinary feats are possible and that something special can emerge from the ordinary.

His largest prospect had never advertised. Most would consider it an unqualified lead, unworthy of attention. But Brian was thinking big, beyond what was evident. He was thinking about what *could be* instead of what *had been*.

Brian's vision was big in another way. Many sellers start small, to break the ice or to keep the initial cost low. Not Brian. He envisioned a breakthrough, both for his territory and for this restaurant.

I wrote up an advertising program for the upcoming year. There were ads for New Year's Eve, Mother's Day, Father's Day, Easter, and so on, complete with taglines for all their holiday ads and ongoing evergreen ads to run weekly in the paper. I'd asked the one artist who was working that week to build out at least twenty ads of different shapes, sizes, and themes. Then I called the restaurant and asked to come in. After a couple of no's, they finally gave me fifteen minutes to share my vision.

I walked in with three poster boards of ad concepts, a detailed plan on how they could run the campaign, and a total cost. I'll never forget the owner's face as I walked through everything. He stopped me and said, "Brian, no one has ever even attempted to do anything like this for us before." No one had ever taken the time to really look at his business and sell him a vision. He signed on the spot that day and those ads ran for many years afterward.

Brian didn't take "no" for an answer because he was emboldened by the power of his vision. He saw it so clearly that he was able to breathe life into it, first with a schedule, then with spec ad designs, and finally with a passionate presentation.

Leaders turn possibilities into opportunities. They imagine that extraordinary feats are possible and that something special can emerge from the ordinary. Leaders give shape and focus to hopes, dreams, and wishes. They make them easier to see and seize. Think of it this way. Imagine you're driving along a coastal highway on a bright, sunny day. The ocean gleams on your right. On some curves, the cliffs plunge hundreds of feet to the water. You can see for miles. You're cruising along, one hand on the wheel, sitting back, tunes blaring, and not a care in the world. You come around a sharp bend in the road and, suddenly, without warning, you're engulfed in a thick fog. What do you do?

We've asked this question many times in workshops and presentations. Here are some of the things people say:

➤ "I slow way down."

➤ "I turn my lights on."

➤ "I tighten my grip on the steering wheel with both hands."

➤ "I tense up."

➤ "I sit up straight or even lean forward."

➤ "I turn the music off."

Soon, you go around another curve in the road. The fog lifts, and it's clear and sunny again. What do you do now? Sit back and relax, speed up, turn the lights off, put the music back on, and enjoy the scenery.

This analogy illustrates how important it is to have clarity of vision. An important part of any seller's job is to lift the fog. You must make the vision so clear that buyers can see the road ahead, relax, pick up speed, and enjoy the ride.

"When I'm purchasing fish from my supplier, he always tells me more than the current market price," one buyer told us about his favorite seller. "He tells me how much the fishermen have caught and what it's looking like for next week on pricing. He's always updating me on new and exciting products that I can test and try." This seller lifts the fog, and shows what's on the road ahead. The seller's information helps with planning and generates ongoing excitement about the future.

To make the possibilities and vision as clear as you can for buyers, there are three things you must do:

☑ Be Specific.

Personalize the possibilities. The vision you share with buyers must be personal, relevant, and meaningful to their future. When there are multiple decision-makers, the vision must be personally meaningful to each one. Every individual needs to see how his or her long-term interests can be realized in this common vision. That unique and ideal image of the future must include specific possibilities that will capture the imagination, and touch the heart, of every individual buyer.

Your company's generic marketing materials can't do this. Testimonials from satisfied customers won't stand alone either. Even the product benefits aren't enough. You need to lead the discussion, weaving these elements together with the most essential part of all—specific possibilities that matter to the buyer and contain a compelling image of what his or her future could be. Only when buyers see their future clearly and completely can they take steps to move forward, with you leading them, toward that vision.

☑ Be Singular in Your Focus.

Give buyers fewer choices and focus on one choice that's exciting and relevant. Instead of talking about all the generic possibilities, create a vision that magnifies one compelling outcome. Buyers shut down when there are too many options. If the effort required to analyze multiple options outweighs the pleasure of the buying experience, buyers won't buy. Your vision must take form as a picture instead of being a kaleidoscope of breathtaking colors.

Numerous studies reveal what happens when buyers have too many choices. In one series of experiments, shoppers in one group were given six gourmet jams to sample, while the second group was given twenty-four varieties to sample. Both groups were given coupons to purchase a jar, and both had all twenty-four varieties to choose from at the point of purchase. Ten times as many people from the first group made a purchase. The group with more choices was overwhelmed and couldn't make a selection.[1]

☑ Be Unwavering in Your Commitment.

Stories from Judith, Brian, and other sellers at their personal best have one thing in common: they consistently attribute their success to persistence. Rightly so. People are inspired by commitment. Often, though, sellers confuse being persistent with being pushy. They stop calling to avoid seeming pushy which, to buyers, appears to be a lack of commitment.

When it comes to bringing possibilities to life, consider the subtle differences between perseverance and persistence. To *persist* means to continue steadfastly. To *persevere* means to purposefully pursue an outcome even in the face of hardship or obstacles. The differences lie in having a purpose that's larger than the relentless activity and in continuing toward that purpose even in the face of adversity. In sales, these differences translate like this: Persistence includes activities like sending weekly "just checking in" emails to a prospect, whereas perseverance involves more effort to doggedly pursue meaningful next steps with a buyer.

Turning persistence into perseverance takes a deeply held belief, a drive and zeal to make something special happen. It takes passion. Angela Duckworth, professor of psychology at the University of Pennsylvania, has a name for this powerful combination of perseverance plus passion in pursuit of long-term goals. She calls it "grit." Her research reveals that most people have more perseverance than passion. Angela measures passion by "consistency over time," not intensity of expression or feeling. It's the endurance, not the enthusiasm, that makes passion part of grit.[2]

> **To make the possibilities and vision clear, be specific, singular in your focus, and unwavering in your commitment.**

For sellers, envisioning the future can turn humdrum persistence into get-you-noticed perseverance. Putting passion into the mix demonstrates commitment. Make the extra efforts to bring the vision to life.

FIND A COMMON PURPOSE

Leaders have a vision and use it to "lift the fog." But exemplary leaders don't develop their vision in isolation and impose it on others. People want to see their own ideals and aspirations, their hopes and dreams, incorporated in the vision. They want to see themselves in the picture of the future the leader is painting.[3] In selling, the central task is inspiring a *shared* vision, not selling your personal ideas and preferred future state. This requires finding common ground with your buyers.

Kyle Hullmann, business development manager for AllSearch Professional Staffing, spent six months wooing a local prospect who had never utilized a search firm. Kyle was diligent in following up. He listed all the benefits of doing business with a search firm, painting the picture of how his local business could source more skilled candidates, do it more quickly, save money, and conserve valuable time and resources that could be devoted to other types of work. After six months, Kyle got word that he'd been very convincing. The prospect had decided to move forward with professional staffing services—but not with Kyle and his company. Instead, they'd opted to contract with a well-known national temp agency.

Kyle was shocked and disheartened. He'd invested a lot of time and felt blindsided. He decided to try once more to win the business. He gave the prospect a complete rundown of competitive advantages only his firm could offer. He shared personal stories and examples. He made an impassioned plea for doing business locally, sourcing local candidates, and keeping the prospect's local business tied to the community's talent pool. He asked for the opportunity to compete head-to-head with the better-known agency to prove his company's capabilities in delivering higher caliber candidates. The buyer agreed, and it took just one round of candidates to confirm Kyle's point. Inspired by the possibilities of doing business that would benefit the local community, the company contracted with AllSearch and Kyle to staff up 25 percent and to find the director's successor, too.

> In selling, the central task is inspiring a *shared* vision, not selling your personal ideas and preferred future state.

Until Kyle took those extra steps, three key ingredients were missing. He hadn't fully demonstrated his credibility and his company's capability compared to a familiar brand. He hadn't made the vision personal to his prospect. And he hadn't asked for commitment and formed a partnership in bringing the vision to life. He was almost out-sold by a seller who had big-name power to wield and, with it, an implied assurance of success. What saved the sale was demonstrating alignment with the buyer's hopes and aspirations.

For Kyle, this was a lesson learned, and an account saved. But similar oversights in creating and conveying a credible and compelling case afflict sellers everywhere. It may be the seller's haste that causes it. Or it could be the seller's desire to presumably save the buyer's time and get right down to business. Often, it's that a seller makes assumptions about the buyer and offers a generalized, product-focused solution instead of an exciting and ennobling vision of the future that includes benefits that are relevant and meaningful to the individual buyer. In any case, the buyer is left out of the vision.

If the big picture doesn't include what the buyer aspires to accomplish, there will be no sale. Buyers want to be heard and understood. As one buyer said, "It has to be about my wants and needs and the company's, too. There has to be respect for my goals, or it's just a standard sales pitch and some product a vendor is trying to pawn off on me." To find the common purpose that will be the lifeblood of your shared vision, there are three things you must do:

☑ Ask the Right Questions.

The right questions are the ones for which you don't already have the answers. Asking questions to corral a buyer into your preconceived vision won't yield buyer commitment or reveal common purpose. Asking questions with a genuine intent to discover and understand what matters to the buyer gives you the raw ingredients of a stirring shared vision.

> **Visions emanate from what buyers share about themselves.**

Asking questions for which you don't have the answers also prevents you from operating on your own assumptions. Not all buyers want the same things for the same reasons. Remaining open to buyer input about the vision will keep you from racing ahead with one of your own.

☑ Listen Actively and Empathetically.

The best leaders are great listeners, as are the most successful sellers.[4] The most effective listening consists of three behaviors: sensing, evaluating, and responding. *Sensing* refers to being fully attuned to verbal and nonverbal cues, including tone, inflection, and expression. *Evaluating* encompasses the logical and emotional assessment of a buyer's words to discover underlying meaning and make connections. *Responding* includes what is conveyed through words, gestures, expressions, and body language. Sellers must engage in all three aspects of listening to be perceived as effective listeners.[5]

You may miss the common purpose and deep-level desires of your buyers if you aren't listening intently, with both your brain and your heart. Visions emanate from what buyers share about themselves. Listen to fully comprehend what buyers want and why they want it, what they value, what they dream about, and what personal meaning they could derive from the vision you're creating with them. In our research about what buyers wanted to see more of from sellers, nearly one-third of the comments pertained to listening, understanding, or showing genuine interest in the buyer.

☑ Get to the Heart of the Matter.

By listening with empathy, you learn what gives meaning and purpose to the work your buyers do. Like all people, buyers want to be pursuing meaningful purpose, not just exchanging their work for cash. People have a deep desire to make a difference. They want to know they've done something worthwhile, that there's a purpose for their existence.[6] To be a leader and sell more effectively, you must put principles and purpose ahead of everything else. That's what calls your buyers to action and ensures they stay the course. People commit to causes, not plans. A vision for the future is much more likely to get a "yes" than a proposed solution. Lead your buyers toward a purpose-driven vision instead of selling them a product-based solution.

 Sellers who indicate that they paint the big picture with buyers about what they hope to accomplish feel more effective in their jobs.

To engage buyers in a shared vision, you must find a common purpose. A two-way dialogue about the future surfaces more than the obvious business needs. As a leader, you elevate your sales approach to inspiring a shared vision by gathering more than the transactional data required for a mere purchase. You're making it personal, creating an awesome connecting experience.

Take Action: Envision the Future

To Envision the Future, imagine exciting and ennobling possibilities. This means you must:

1. Determine what you care about, what drives you, where your passions lie, and why you wish to accomplish the goals you've set.

2. Be curious about what's going on around you and ask "What's next?" about every interaction with a buyer. Don't wait until renewal time or routine checkpoints.

3. Listen to your buyers about what is important to their future, both professionally and personally.

4. Involve others in crafting the exciting possibilities that you could bring to life together. Don't make this a unilateral process.

5. Get people on the same page and on the same path about where you all are going together.

6 | ENLIST OTHERS

AS VICE PRESIDENT OF SALES FOR MODUS ENGAGEMENT,
Adam Luckeroth oversees complex sales with long sales cycles involving dozens of people whose efforts must be coordinated. With one high-value prospect, he spent time nurturing a relationship with an individual who wasn't the decision-maker. She helped Adam by making introductions to key decision-makers in the IT, sales, and marketing departments, advocating for people to meet with Adam, and coaching him on the people he'd meet. It took time, but finally some doors began to open, and "we got a small deal done," Adam told us.

> *In software, it's all about "land and expand." Over the next two years, she and I worked closely together, and she was the true definition of an internal champion. I supported her, and she started doing more and more selling internally. Last year, she won a prestigious award because of our platform and what it was doing for the organization. While I worked hard, she worked harder and used our platform to raise her profile in a very large corporation.*

Adam earned the support of this internal champion by tapping into something meaningful to her. She was looking for an opportunity to stand out in a highly competitive sea of talent. He realized he could help her and was able, therefore, to enlist her in his vision for her corporation's marketing and sales teams.

> **Visionary leaders don't rally support by saying "Join me in doing the ordinary; let's go do what everyone else is doing!"**

Part of enlisting others is finding common ground. Equally important is the passion leaders express for the vision. Buyers expect sellers to be *inspiring*. They use words like *enthusiastic, excited, confident*, and *passionate* to describe their best-in-class sellers. When buyers talk about sellers they prefer to buy from, they say things like "If a seller *truly* believes, I will, too" and "The way they demonstrate lets us know how much they care about our interests and needs."

The most productive sellers indicate that they are nearly always communicating with genuine conviction, and with the big picture in mind.

It takes vast reserves of energy and excitement for people to sustain commitment to a distant dream. They aren't going to follow someone who's only mildly enthusiastic about future possibilities. People actively support those who are *wildly* enthusiastic.

When you're trying to mobilize a buying team or a single buyer, to *Enlist Others* you must act on these two essentials:

- **Appeal to common ideals**
- **Animate the vision**

Those sellers who are in the top third of the distribution on Enlist Others are 87 percent more likely to agree that they are effective in meeting the demands of their work than those in the bottom third of the distribution. Moreover, sellers in the top third of the frequency distribution report their productivity as more than four times higher than those in the bottom third, and still nearly two times higher than those in the middle of the distribution.

Enlisting others is all about igniting passion for a purpose and moving people to persevere against great odds. To get extraordinary things done for your buyers, and with your buyers, you have to go beyond logic, engaging the hearts as well as the minds of everyone involved. You start by understanding their strongest yearnings for something meaningful and significant.

APPEAL TO COMMON IDEALS

Leaders reach for the ideal. They set out to achieve something beyond good. They aim for something extraordinary. They're ambitious and optimistic. Visionary leaders don't rally support by saying, "Join me in doing the ordinary; let's go do what everyone else is doing!" In selling, your vision must stretch to the ideal so that it will encompass exciting possibilities, breakthrough innovations, and revolutionary changes to the status quo.

When you communicate a vision to your buyers and others who will bring it to life, you'll talk about something much bigger than a product solution. You'll talk about the difference they will make, the impact they will have, and the higher meaning and purpose of the work ahead. You must show every individual how his or her long-term interests can be realized by enlisting in a common vision. You need to describe a compelling image of what the future could be like when people join in a common cause.[1]

Consider this example. Two paper shredding companies compete for corporate accounts in a busy metropolitan area. Both offer mobile shredding for on-site document destruction. They both offer premium options like video capture to create an indisputable record of the document handling. They are equivalent in their compliance with federal privacy laws. Both companies are at the same price point per pound of shredded paper, and their response time and other service offerings are virtually identical. There doesn't seem to be a competitive advantage for either company. So why was Melanie able to outsell Marcus at such an alarming rate where their territories overlapped? Why was Melanie's company rapidly gaining market share? Marcus was stumped.

When Marcus asked former buyers why they weren't renewing agreements with him, they gave vague responses. He wondered whether there was something shady going on or, perhaps, Melanie was offering a top-secret price cut to steal his customers. Marcus convinced his boss to fight fire with fire. They developed a special offer with a discounted rate. It attracted a few new buyers, but the biggest ones they'd lost still seemed uninterested. So Marcus and his sales manager cut costs again and added a new rapid response offering. With expense costs rising and top-line revenue eroding, profitability nosedived. The company soon learned that adjusting prices back up was considerably more difficult than reducing them. Melanie's company, meanwhile, continued promoting the original rate and continued to grow market share.

In desperation, before his company went out of business, Marcus applied for a sales role at Melanie's expanding company. In his third week, after new hire orientation and developing a required prospect list, Marcus shadowed another seller to learn the company's go-to-market strategy. He immediately noticed there were no top-secret price cuts or tricky tactics. There was, however, an entirely different sales approach than the one his former employer had utilized.

In his former job, Marcus identified top prospects by type and size of business. He knew medical and legal offices had to follow specific laws governing document handling, so he focused primarily on them. He opened by asking qualifying questions about the volume of shredding needed, frequency preferred, the sensitivity of the information, privacy concerns, and the need for video documentation. Once he scoped the opportunity, he presented his company's offering of services, guarantees, and prices. He won deals, he thought, by being honest, affable, and knowledgeable about privacy laws.

With his new employer, Marcus was taught to start by visiting a prospect's website and learning about their mission and values. The ones that listed "sustainability" or "protecting the environment" or "respecting privacy" were classified as top, A-level prospects, regardless of business type. If a company's website didn't contain phrases like those, the prospect was classified as a B or C, depending on size. Most of the doctors and attorneys Marcus had considered "no brainers" were rated as C's. That didn't make sense to him. He was skeptical about calling on A-rated prospects like light industrial plants, technology companies, and corporate offices. He believed they wouldn't have enough volume to justify contracted services and that they wouldn't see the need to pay for shredding since they could just throw non-sensitive material in trash or recycling bins.

Week three was the turning point. As Marcus observed sales calls to HR, security, risk management, and other departments, he realized he'd been thinking too narrowly about prospect opportunities. More importantly, he witnessed an entirely different way to sell. The seller he shadowed didn't ask qualifying questions about volume and frequency. Those details only came up when they wrote the contract. Instead, the seller consulted his notes about each company's mission and values to craft his opening question. In three calls, Marcus heard variations of the same question:

> ➤ "I noticed that one of your company values is to 'build confidence and trust in all interactions.' I was wondering what that means to you and the work you do."
> ➤ "I noticed that your company mission is 'to stand up for economic and social progress.' How does the work you do represent that?"
> ➤ "I noticed that your purpose statement says this company empowers communities 'to drive real and lasting change.' In what ways do you contribute to this aim?"

Marcus noticed how all prospects reacted similarly. They paused, smiled or nodded, relaxed a bit, and gave detailed and impassioned answers. They linked three things together: their roles, their contributions to the company, and something of personal value. For example, the plant facilities manager for a company that promoted economic and social progress shared that he recently joined co-workers in a rally against immigration policy changes. He said, "I literally stood up to something I don't like, and it felt good to do that." He described how his job is behind the scenes and how he sometimes feels invisible, but the protest was a way for him to stand up publicly for something that mattered to him.

Marcus also observed how his new sales colleague listened carefully to people's responses and found ways to align naturally with their ideals and values. Soon after the facilities plant manager proudly described the immigration rally, the seller asked: "What would it mean to you if you could stand up for something important every single day, something small that made a big difference?"

The manager leaned in. He didn't respond right away, but his interest was piqued. The seller said, "You can, you know. Even behind the scenes you already make a difference to the people here who count on you. But you can also make a difference for future generations. Just as you're fighting to protect the rights of immigrants, you can protect the rights we all have to a clean and healthy planet." Then he stopped. There was a long pause.

"You sell shredding services, right?" the plant manager finally asked. "So you're saying if I shred instead of recycling that I'm going to make some kind of impact?"

Exemplary leaders don't impose their visions of the future on people; they liberate the vision that's already stirring in their constituents.

With that, the seller finished painting the picture. He described recycling processes in detail and explained how nearly 100 percent of shredded material is recycled in environmentally friendly ways. He told a story about reducing the destruction of virgin forests. He described the benefits of using shredded paper as mulch to improve soil quality and crop yield in impoverished areas, and the importance of using shredded paper for packing in place of environmentally unfriendly Styrofoam. In his four years selling these services, Marcus had never known how important shredding was. The buyer was equally impressed, especially when the seller said, "This is what you can impact. All of this is how you can fight the good fight every single day to protect the rights of future generations. Let me show you how easy it is for you to stand up and make that impact."

This seller knew how to connect to what's meaningful to others. He created an awesome connecting experience by asking an opening question that dignified the buyer and drew out personal sharing about values and purpose. This seller found common purpose and appealed to common ideals, all in a matter of minutes.

Exemplary leaders don't impose their visions of the future on people; they liberate the vision that's already stirring in their constituents. They awaken dreams, breathe life into them, and arouse the belief that people can achieve something grand. It's the same in selling. You must have a purpose, and you must connect it to your buyer's ideals.

ANIMATE THE VISION

Part of motivating others is appealing to their ideals. Another part is animating the vision and breathing life into it. To enlist others, you need to help them *see* and *feel* how their interests and aspirations align with the vision. In sales, the classic example of this is the test drive. The reason sellers want car shoppers to get behind the wheel and take it for a spin right away is simple. There's no better way to *see* and *feel* what it would be like to own that vehicle than by driving it.

Without a tangible, test-drivable product, you must paint a compelling picture of the future, one that is so vivid and specific that buyers know exactly what it would be like to live and work in that exciting and uplifting future state. That's the only way they will be sufficiently motivated to commit their time, energy, and sustained focus to the vision's realization. Animating the vision makes it so real and meaningful that people will boldly act to do their part in advancing toward it.

You may not think of yourself as expressive or emotional enough to paint a word picture that would give people this kind of courage and commitment. You may not see yourself as someone who can speak with genuine conviction about the meaning and purpose of your work with your buyers. You may think you work with buyers who want facts and figures, minus the fluff. The truth is that everyone is capable of speaking expressively and convincingly, and you do it more often than you realize or appreciate.

 There's a positive correlation between the frequency with which sellers speak with genuine conviction about the higher meaning and purpose of their work and both their sense of pride in the work they do and their productivity.

When you *believe* strongly in something, you naturally speak in an impassioned way to communicate what you feel. Your passion brings it to life. Your enthusiasm and expressiveness come from your beliefs. When you unleash your enthusiasm and expressiveness, you muster commitment and courage in others. Don't underestimate your talents.

Don't let your talents be diluted, either, by canned sales presentations that are packed full of data and product features. Details derail sales. Buyers want to be stirred into action. American architect and urban designer Daniel Burnham understood this. When he was eulogized by his arch rival Frank Lloyd Wright as "an enthusiastic promoter of great construction enterprises," Wright spoke to Burnham's sales abilities more than his architectural style, and said, "His powerful personality was supreme."[2]

> **When you weave the emotional connection to what matters most to the buyer together with the logical case for change, you animate the vision.**

This visionary architect didn't rely on blueprints, sketches, drafts, and plans. Burnham surely had all of those in hand, but he didn't lead with them. Instead, in describing his "city of the future" master plan for Chicago, he spoke from his heart about what he'd pictured for his hometown. He used imagery, descriptive words, and the interests and dreams of those to whom he was talking to inspire the city's movers and shakers to support the plan. Sellers in any sector can do the same.

When you weave the emotional connection to what matters most to the buyer together with the logical case for change, you animate the vision. You breathe life into it by making it more concrete. To accomplish this, leaders use symbolic language to create mental pictures and provide something familiar that makes a vision seem more real. They tell stories and share anecdotes to connect the elements of the vision and portray what it will look like as it takes shape. They offer examples and testimonials to draw parallels between something proven in the past and an image of the future. All of this helps buyers, too, to picture the possibilities.

Metaphors have this power. A metaphor is a figure of speech used to show a resemblance to something that is not actually the same. "You ain't nothin' but a hound dog," "all the world's a stage," and "the elephant in the room" are metaphors that conjure up instant images and elicit comparisons to promote understanding. Marc Benioff, CEO of Salesforce, is a master of metaphors. He includes "make your own metaphors" as one of the crucial plays that contributed to the explosive growth of Salesforce from a little idea to a company worth $8 billion in under twenty years. Marc says metaphors are a great way to communicate your message: "I spend a lot of time creating metaphors to explain what we do. For example, early on I explained what we did with the metaphor 'salesfoce.com is Amazon.com meets Siebel Systems.' Later, when we launched AppExchange, we called it 'the eBay of enterprise software.'"[3]

People are twenty-two times more likely to remember a fact when it has been wrapped in a story.

Relating something new to something familiar creates a feeling of comfort. Symbolic language and comparisons help people see what you're proposing. With a little practice, you can create your own powerful metaphors. They're all around you, and you probably use them already. There are art metaphors, game and sports metaphors, war metaphors, science fiction metaphors, machine metaphors, religious metaphors, and spiritual metaphors. James Geary, deputy curator at the Nieman Foundation for Journalism at Harvard University and a leading expert on the use of metaphorical language, reports that people use a metaphor every ten to twenty-five words, or about six metaphors a minute.[4] Learning to intentionally use metaphors and other symbolic language greatly enhances your ability to enlist others in a common vision of the future.

Storytelling is another way to infuse facts with meaning and connect the dots between emotions and logic. Educational psychologist Jerome Bruner determined that people are twenty-two times more likely to remember a fact when it has been wrapped in a story.[5] This is why television commercials and letters from charitable organizations show you the stories of people your donations can help instead of giving you the simple facts about the need. When you can relate emotionally to the story, you are more likely to respond. Stories invite listeners to travel somewhere new with you, from "once upon a time" to "happily ever after." When we listen to stories, we are engaged and feel a sense of belonging. This buyer's simple statement sums up the importance of telling stories: "I appreciate personal stories because it helps to build not only a business relationship but a personal one as well. It has a huge impact as it builds trust and creates a partnership."

A vision is an image in the mind. A vision becomes real as you translate images into concrete and relatable form for your buyers. The word *vision* itself stems from the root word "to see." Vision statements, then, are not statements at all. They are pictures. They are images of the future.

This means to enlist others in a shared vision, you must be able to speak about the future and create pictures with words so buyers have a mental image of what things will be like when they embark on this quest with you. You have to use descriptive phrases and specific examples to deliver the mental image a buyer can relate to and see. This is not a skill reserved for a few gifted speakers. This is something you already do when you genuinely want people to understand things the way you do.

Think about something you enjoy doing. When you describe your hobby to someone else, you speak descriptively and share specific examples. You create mental images by using words alone. How you say them matters, too. Social scientists have found that individuals who are perceived as charismatic are simply more animated than people who are not perceived that way. They smile more, speak faster, pronounce words more clearly, and move their heads and bodies more often. Being energetic and expressive are the keys to being perceived as someone who is charismatic. Humor and energetic interaction add to the perception.[6] The old saying that enthusiasm is contagious is certainly true for sellers.

Speak about the future and create pictures with words so buyers have a mental image of what things will be like when they embark on this quest with you.

Creating a mental image, telling stories, and using descriptive language all trigger emotional responses. These techniques for animating the vision simultaneously produce an awesome connecting experience infused with meaning and emotional sway for your buyers. Your commitment and conviction will shine through as you appeal to common ideals and enlist others to animate the vision.

Take Action: Enlist Others

Enlist Others in a common vision by appealing to shared aspirations. This means you need to:

1. Talk with your buyers and find out about their hopes, dreams, and aspirations for the future.

2. Show that you listen to what they say by incorporating their input.

3. Make sure your buyers know and take pride in what makes the solution you've worked on together unique and special.

4. Show your buyers how their long-term interests are served by enlisting in a common vision.

5. Use metaphors, stories, testimonials, examples, word pictures, and demonstrations to make the vision of the future something relatable, concrete, and real.

CHALLENGE THE PROCESS

Ask any seller about a personal-best sales experience, and you'll hear three elements in the story: it wasn't easy, it required perseverance, and it needed a unique or creative approach to make it happen. You might expect sellers to select personal bests based on highest dollar sales or sales that earned them the most recognition. Sometimes those rewards are footnotes in sellers' personal-best stories, but seldom is the payoff the reason why the seller selected a particular experience. Instead, it's the challenge and how he or she overcame it that a seller focused on most.

Challenge is a fertile breeding ground for greatness. People do their best when there's the chance to change the way things are. Maintaining the status quo simply breeds mediocrity and, in sales, is a surefire way to lose an account to a competitor who offers something new and exciting. Exemplary sellers seek and accept challenging opportunities to test their abilities. They motivate buyers and internal partners, too, to test themselves and exceed their self-imposed limits. Leaders seize initiative and make something meaningful happen.

Leaders set the stage for greatness, but leadership is not a solo act. Sellers who shared their successes credited entire teams with the changes that resulted in extraordinary outcomes. Exemplary sellers look for good ideas everywhere—from members of their own teams, their buyers' teams, and any other resource that can spark a new way of thinking. Leaders listen, take advice, and learn continuously.

Progress is not made in giant leaps; it's made incrementally. Exemplary leaders move forward in small steps with little victories, something sellers are generally accustomed to in advancing any sale. They turn adversity into advantage and setbacks into successes. They persevere with grit and determination. Leaders also venture out. They test and they take risks with bold ideas. And because risk taking involves mistakes and failure, leaders accept the inevitable disappointments and treat them as opportunities for learning and growth.

As an exemplary leader, you will engage in the leadership practice of *Challenge the Process* when you

- **Search for opportunities by seizing the initiative and looking outward for innovative ways to improve.**
- **Experiment and take risks by consistently generating small wins and learning from experience.**

7 | SEARCH FOR OPPORTUNITIES

WHEN THE U.S. DEPARTMENT OF DEFENSE CALLED, it was a matter of national security. Ted Heiman could hardly believe what he was hearing. The Defense Manpower Data Center (DMDC) had an urgent need to implement a new, more secure I.D. badge for 4.3 million active duty service members. Two Secret Service agents had used fake military I.D. badges to enter the Pentagon and access the Attorney General's office while wearing their firearms. The Joint Chiefs stepped in and issued an order to fix this problem immediately.

Ted understood the urgency: "If they were able to enter the Pentagon, they could access any U.S. military base on the planet. The situation was unacceptable." Ted was intrigued by the magnitude of the problem and the size of the opportunity. But this would be no small feat, he said.

The technical solution they were looking for did not exist. Their vision was far ahead of most corporate enterprises. The U.S. military needed a new way to authenticate soldiers to military bases and networks around the world, incorporating biometrics and other technologies, while making it virtually impossible to counterfeit the credential. Beyond the technology challenges, the politics between all the agencies involved in the project was staggering, including the DMDC, the National Security Agency, the Defense Information Systems Agency, plus the Army, Navy, and Air Force. Each had its own competing priorities.

On top of these requirements, we were told we couldn't change any of the existing technologies on the old cardboard laminated I.D. badge or the systems they currently interfaced with including the Real-Time Automated Personnel Identification System (RAPIDS) used to issue the old IF badge. Most sales people would have walked away. It was too big and too hard, and the solution did not exist. It had never been done before.

Even though Ted's company, ActivIdentity, was a small security start-up at that time, he gathered the technical team together and started the daunting task of creating a complete identity management solution. Some of the core components were already in development, but the solution had never been deployed to such a large user community. Ted would not only have to take some serious risks, but he would also need to look outside his firm for expertise. He contacted partners in other companies he'd worked with in the past. Each had a critical piece of the puzzle, but the diverse technologies had never been integrated. Everyone involved would need to stretch beyond his or her current capabilities and collaborate to create the solution. The project would be an uphill struggle due to the strict security requirements, the innovative technology, and the politics between agencies.

After several conversations with his partners, Ted called the DMDC. He told them, "We have a high level of confidence that we can pull this deal off, but it will require a great deal of development work and will be very expensive." They asked him what it would cost to create a "proof of concept" (POC) and how quickly they could demonstrate it. "Three months and $500,000," Ted said. They gave the project an immediate go-ahead. Ted and his team delivered the POC on time and were awarded a single source contract. The DOD has invested over $30 million dollars to date in the CAC Card Project. The combined team also would win the Gracie—the Government Technology Leadership award for its impact and garner Ted a letter of commendation acknowledging the critical role he played in bringing all the various parties together to protect national security.

Sometimes challenges find leaders, and sometimes leaders find challenges; most often, it's a little of each, as in Ted's situation. What Ted did is what all exemplary leaders do. He looked outward, keeping up with changing trends and remaining sensitive to external realities. He persuaded others to take seriously the challenges and opportunities they faced. He served as a catalyst for change, challenging the way they did things and convincing others they needed new practices to succeed.

> **The more that sellers report that they search outside the formal boundaries of their organization for innovative ways to improve, the clearer they are about what's expected of them, and the more motivated they are to work as hard as they can to do their jobs well.**

In today's competitive marketplace, business-as-usual thinking is ineffective, and exemplary sellers know they must transform the way things are done. You cannot deliver extraordinary results with good intentions alone. Change requires that you actively seek ways to make things better—to grow, to innovate, and to improve.

Exemplary sellers embrace the commitment to *Search for Opportunities* to make extraordinary things happen. They make sure they engage in these two essentials:

- **Seize the initiative**
- **Exercise outsight**

Sometimes, you have to shake things up. Other times, you just have to harness the uncertainty that surrounds you. Regardless, to make new things happen, you must rely on outsight to actively seek innovative ideas from beyond the boundaries of familiar experience.

SEIZE THE INITIATIVE

Meeting new challenges requires doing things differently. The study of leadership is the study of how men and women guide others through adversity, uncertainty, and other significant challenges. It's the story of people like Ted who triumph against overwhelming odds, who take initiative, who confront the established order, who mobilize individuals and institutions in the face of stiff resistance. Leadership, challenge, and seizing the initiative are all linked together.

> **If you aren't differentiating yourself as a change maker, restless buyers will look elsewhere for new ideas.**

That's why buyers stick with sellers who demonstrate leadership in the face of challenges. Comments like these from our buyer study affirm how important it is to recognize the opportunities you will have to stand out:

➤ "The seller really got creative to solve a challenging business need. Doing so created a win-win situation and deepened the partnering relationship."

➤ "The product had an issue, and the seller was helpful, fixing it by listening and being open and honest."

➤ "The seller came up with new solutions to prevent a problem from happening again. It made me feel both grateful and less stressed."

Taking charge of change is one way to seize the initiative. Buyers certainly appreciate responsiveness when there's a problem. Leaders, however, are proactive. They don't wait for problems or for things to go wrong. Instead, they anticipate them and work ahead to prevent them. When there are no problems to anticipate, leaders look for ways to make improvements. They identify what could be better by asking why things are the way they are. They don't settle for the status quo because they know that complacency breeds mediocrity.

Sellers can't risk standing still. The competitive threat is too great, and B2B buyers aren't as loyal as they used to be.[1] If you aren't differentiating yourself as a change maker, restless buyers will look elsewhere for new ideas.

Positive comments from the buyer surveys about proactive sellers outnumbered comments about problem-solving sellers two-to-one. Buyers expect sellers to do both: to take initiative in anticipating *and* in responding to changes, but they give higher praise to sellers who get ahead of problems and lead change. For example:

- ➤ "When I've got a seller who knows what I need and can anticipate and predetermine what I'm going to need, that's great."
- ➤ "The sellers take initiative in anticipating and responding to changes. It makes me feel that they are smart and put together when they take extra effort to think toward the future in a constructive way."
- ➤ "One seller did research for me that was not expected. He wanted to learn more about the process and took time to visit. As a result, his solutions are more pertinent to our needs, and I trust him to find what I need. He's very proactive."
- ➤ "It is very important to me that the seller look for innovative ways to improve because my business is ever-changing and not always flexible. When a rare seller does this, I continue to use her services or products."

You may never get a chance with a buyer unless you've shown your ability to seize the initiative.

There's no need to wait for permission to take initiative to help your buyers. Jump right in and make something happen. You may never have a chance with a buyer unless you've shown your ability to seize the initiative. Going the extra distance will differentiate you and demonstrate your commitment.

When you Challenge the Process, however, be sure you are challenging with purpose. Challenging isn't effective as a ploy to get the buyer's attention. In recent years, this has become a common misapplication of The Challenger® Sale methodology. The original recommendation from this research was that sellers be "assertive, pushing back when necessary and taking control of the sale rather than acquiescing to the customer's every demand or objection."[2] Some sellers take this too far, using their interpretation of this approach as a license to be confrontational with buyers. At a 2017 Sales 3.0 conference, one speaker brought down the house when he said, "I can't take any more arrogant, 26-year-old, challenger selling, know-it-alls telling me I don't know how to run my own business. Can someone just teach the Challenger Sales crowd some manners?"

> **Exemplary sellers, like leaders, challenge with purpose because they have the drive to make things better.**

The misunderstandings about that research and the backlash it's producing are unfortunate. There are aspects of The Challenger Sale research that buyers in our study unknowingly reinforced. The four hallmarks of a Challenger seller[3] were positively viewed by the buyers we surveyed:

➤ **Always Has a Different View of the World.** "Creativity and passion make a seller's ideas more interesting to me."

➤ **Understands the Customer's Business.** "I need a two-way conversation that shows they're trying to learn my needs and understand our objectives."

➤ **Loves to Debate.** "I like someone who thinks outside the box and challenges others to do the same."

➤ **Pushes the Customer.** "It's good to get opinions, even if I don't agree."

At the same time, buyers clearly conveyed that these qualities are not the ones they favored most. Sales organizations are, unfortunately, "putting all their eggs in one basket" if hiring and training exclusively from The Challenger Sale recommendations.

Buyers are looking for leadership that includes *purposeful* challenging, but the seller must offer more to back up challenges made. By first establishing credibility, finding shared values and common purpose, and building a trust-based relationship, sellers have more leeway when it comes time for challenging buyers.

Exemplary sellers, like leaders, challenge with purpose because they have the drive to make things better. They challenge, usually with great passion, because they fervently believe they can improve the status quo and help buyers realize their visions. For buyers to be fully engaged in the challenge, they need to know why you are issuing the challenge. The purpose infuses the process and pain of change with meaning. When people see the meaning, they are more willing to deal with the uncertainty and complexity of change. If you are asking your buyers to make a change, you're asking them to struggle willingly. Change is hard. The reason for it needs to be more than a short-term benefit. It has to be something more uplifting so it can sustain buyers through the period of struggle. Be sure to connect the challenge to the greater good and give your buyers a reason to care and commit to it.

EXERCISE OUTSIGHT

Leaders purposefully challenge themselves, too. They are on a continual quest to find new ideas and new ways of looking at the world. They strive to innovate and know it's self-limiting to look only inward for determining what's new, what's next, and what's better. Innovation comes from using outsight. *Insight* is the ability to apprehend the inner nature of things. By contrast, *outsight* is the awareness and understanding of outside forces. You can't have outsight without openness. If you want to use outsight, you always need to be receptive to ideas from buyers, suppliers, internal partners, end users, competitors, and colleagues. You never know what may spark an idea.

Ted's success stemmed, in part, from his outsight. "We couldn't do it alone. We needed the brainpower and capabilities of others, including our competitors, to make this happen. It would be too limiting to try to do everything alone. Besides, where's the fun or the learning opportunity in that?"

Buyers appreciate when sellers exercise outsight. One grateful buyer told us that they were unable to solve a problem independently but encountered a seller who "looked and looked and looked for something that would work. And he looked until he found it." This was a major reason they continued purchasing from that seller and company.

One barrier to outsight is confining yourself inside an echo chamber. It may be comforting to surround yourself with like-minded

---

You always need to be receptive to ideas from buyers, suppliers, internal partners, end users, competitors, and colleagues.

---

people who agree with you and endorse your ideas. However, turning to people who see things the way you do and usually agree with you means you'll miss out on ideas outside of the mold. When you seek affirmation instead of a challenge to your thinking, you lose healthy discourse that could reveal new (and potentially better) ways of looking at a situation.

Outsight can help you avoid these limitations. Leaders mine for dissenting and diverse views to circumvent their natural inclinations toward confirmation bias. Sometimes referred to as "myside bias," this is the tendency to search for, interpret, favor, and recall information in a way that confirms pre-existing beliefs or ideas.[4] Because of confirmation bias, people also interpret information in ways that support their own ideas and beliefs. They do not seek information that would disprove what they believe, and they are not discerning when they find information that upholds what they believe.[5] This means that most people are not as good as they think they are at analyzing a situation or making decisions objectively.

Making assumptions about buyers' needs happens all the time in selling. Sellers often have a preconceived notion of what product or solution will work best for a buyer. As the buyer describes his or her needs, the seller subconsciously filters what's being said and mentally prioritizes the information that confirms what the seller set out to sell. Not incorporating the inconvenient information—that which doesn't match the desired outcome—may cause the seller to inadvertently steer the buyer toward a partial solution or, worse, one that is altogether wrong.

When people have a potential for gain or loss, they are even more prone to confirmation bias than when there are no personal stakes.[6] Since sales conversations, by their very nature, always represent a chance of gain or loss for the seller, it's critical to be cognizant of this bias. Exemplary leaders seek diverse points of view and test their own ways of thinking. They do not stubbornly cling to their ideas or the status quo. While persevering toward their vision, leaders remain open to alternative paths that will get them there.

To remain open in this way, leaders take deliberate actions. They ask questions. They encourage idea sharing. They welcome feedback and input. They avoid becoming entrenched in a particular way of thinking or working. They model to others that they are actively searching for innovative ways to improve how work is done. Wharton business school professor Adam Grant refers to this as "creative destruction." He says, "The hallmark of originality is rejecting the default and exploring whether a better option exists." Adam's research provides a valuable starting point for leaders: Be curious. Asking questions like "Why does the default exist in the first place?" can keep you from operating in a constant holding pattern. The objective of asking

---

While persevering toward their vision, leaders remain open to alternative paths that will get them there.

---

questions like this is to develop *vuja de* skills. *Vuja de,* Adam explains, is the opposite of *déjà vu. Déjà vu* occurs when you're experiencing something new but have a sense you've experienced it before. *Vuja de* occurs when you encounter something familiar but are able to see it with a fresh perspective.[7]

Finding a fresh perspective demands moving past your own confirmation bias. You have to force yourself to acknowledge pre-existing views and then seek differing ones. You have to develop a genuine desire to know more and to be interested in the world around you. You have to condition yourself to notice and explore things you don't understand. Being curious, genuinely interested, and open to different viewpoints gives sellers multiple advantages:

> ➤ **Buyers Are Drawn to Sellers Who Show Genuine Interest in Them.** They praise and reward those sellers: "I appreciate when a seller takes a genuine interest in making our company better. That's a big factor in deciding who to give my time to."

> ➤ **Being Inquisitive and Curious Helps Sellers Learn About Business, the Marketplace, and Buyers.** As sellers sate their own curiosity, they're also boosting their credibility and adding value for buyers. As one buyer told us, "I appreciate knowledgeable sellers because I can have confidence when working with them."

> ➤ **Asking Questions and Gathering Information About Buyers Builds Trust and Makes a Seller a Valued Partner.** One buyer described how this works for her: "She really listens and helps me come up with ideas to make things work better. I don't know where we'd be without her."

Curiosity is the gateway to bigger-picture thinking. As you pursue a shared vision with your buyers and internal partners, you'll enrich the meaning and purpose every time you explore the nuances and facets that

You have to force yourself to acknowledge pre-existing views and then seek differing ones.

are revealed. Your passion for the vision will grow if you remain open to the adventure. And it is, indeed, an adventure if you allow it to be. Think of yourself as an explorer, looking for undiscovered ways of doing things. Set out on an exploration of your own company. As you discover how things work in other departments and gather ideas and information from people you seldom spend time with, discipline yourself to create *vuja de* experiences.

As an explorer, also exercise outsight and curiosity with your buyers. If they're not buying, ask why not. Listen, probe, and seek to understand how you can make improvements that would have an impact on their purchasing decisions. Make idea-gathering and inviting feedback from your buyers a part of your routine. But don't stop there. Explore your competitors' websites and network with them at industry conferences and other functions. Keep your antennae up, no matter where you are. You never know when and where you might find the new ideas that make extraordinary sales happen.

As you demonstrate curiosity and seek diverse perspectives, you're modeling the behaviors and mindset you'd like your buyers to adopt. It's easier to sell ideas and vision to buyers who are themselves curious, inquisitive, interested, and open to new ideas. As a leader, you can stimulate this kind of thinking and openness by asking thought-provoking questions. You can engage your buyers in brainstorming and other activities that create an awesome connecting experience at the same time they expand a buyer's thinking and perspective.

You can even make it fun and engaging for buyers as Debby Camalo does. Debby is an account director for TGI Direct, a technology

Exercise outsight and curiosity with your buyers and competitors.

services firm. She is always on the lookout for new ideas and is not afraid to take initiative and make things happen. Debby had been calling on a prospect for more than six months, never making it past the gatekeeper. She had tried every technique she knew to get to the decision-maker. She knew she'd have to be creative and, she figured, she had nothing to lose by taking one last shot.

I decided to deliver a pineapple every day for two weeks straight. Just a pineapple. No note, no explanation. At the beginning of the third week, I showed up and said, "Hello, it's the Pineapple Lady here to see Mr. Madison." He saw me because he was curious and just had to know who was delivering all those pineapples and why.

What can you do with your buyers to make something extraordinary happen? More of the same isn't likely to produce change. That's why you must always be on the watch for a new approach, a new idea, or a new way to get where you're trying to go.

8 | EXPERIMENT AND TAKE RISKS

MADDIE FLETCHER KNOWS EXACTLY HOW LONG it took for one beverage company to give her a chance: 198 days. During that time, Maddie doggedly emailed, called, dropped by, and texted regularly. She knew her company could succeed where multiple suppliers had failed. She just needed a chance to prove it.

Her prospect had only been in business a year, offering fresh, full-flavored craft beverages with all-natural ingredients and no GMOs. The founders' vision was to support nonprofit and community events to uplift and unite people. But first they needed a package design that would get them into retail outlets and consumers' hands. They had a great design concept. They just couldn't find a supplier who could bring their vision to life.

After working with several packaging, labeling, and printing companies, they turned to Maddie and were interested in seeing what her family-owned company could do to create expressive package decoration leading to meaningful consumer brand awareness. After six months of frustrating trial and error with other suppliers, this buyer was relieved to find a seller like Maddie.

The hurdle for other suppliers was applying the label the way they wanted. It was to be thin, form-fitting to their uniquely shaped bottle, vibrant, tamper proof, and providing 360-degree coverage with a seam

that was precisely positioned and barely visible. These custom speci-
fications were usually for high-volume orders, but this company was
selling just 30,000 units a year.

Maddie went to work with the design team on form, fit, and function. Despite the low volume, they designed a full-body shrink sleeve to
fit the bottle size and shape. The sleeve covered the entire bottle, top to
bottom, with perfect seam placement. They approached this challenge
as engineers would; testing each modification along the way. They ex-
perimented and went back to the drawing board several times. They
used a full array of quality assurance tools, involving a series of testing
and inspection processes. They verified density and depth of color to
scientifically match the color and ink impression and then tested each
color in a full range of lighting environments to be certain it was precisely and consistently what the buyer wanted.

This effort was exactly what the buyer had been hoping for. The
look, feel, and vibe of the bottle was everything they'd imagined.
Thanks, in part, to the packaging design, sales the following year sur-
passed 100,000 bottles. Because of the job's complexity, Maddie's company won a prestigious industry award, given to only eight other labels
from around the world.

To achieve the extraordinary, you must be willing, like Maddie, to
do things that have never been done before. You have to investigate
unproven strategies. You have to break out of the norms that box you
in, venture beyond the limitations you usually place on yourself and
others, try new things, and take chances.

 **There's a statistically significant relationship between the
extent that sellers report that they *experiment and take
risks, even when there is a chance of failure,* and their productivity. Those who most frequently engage in this leadership behavior report a productivity rate that is three to
four times that reported by sellers at the other end of the
continuum.**

Leaders take this one step further. Not only are they willing to test
bold ideas and take calculated risks, but they also get others to join

them on these adventures in uncertainty. The difference between an exemplary leader and an individual risk taker is that leaders create the conditions under which people *want* to join them in the struggle.

> **Each advancing step a buyer makes through your pipeline represents a small win.**

Paradoxically, leaders make risk safe. They turn experiments into learning opportunities. They position change as putting one foot in front of the other, step-by-step, toward the vision rather than employing bet-the-company tactics or taking foolhardy actions.

Exemplary leaders make the commitment to *Experiment and Take Risks*. They know it's essential to

- **Generate small wins**
- **Learn from experience**

These essentials help you transform challenge into an exploration, uncertainty into an adventure, fear into resolve, and risk into reward. They are the keys to making progress that becomes unstoppable.

GENERATE SMALL WINS

Leaders dream big but start small. They set milestones along the way to measure progress and keep the project moving forward. They celebrate incremental victories along the way and generate momentum with *small wins*. A small win is defined as "a concrete, complete, implemented outcome of moderate importance."[1] Small wins make big projects seem doable. They minimize the risk of trying and reduce the costs of failing. Once people achieve a small win and feel successful, it sets in motion natural forces that build momentum and favors progress over setbacks.

As a seller, you know the benefits of small wins. Each advancing step a buyer makes through your pipeline represents a small win. Each micro-commitment a buyer makes—to research your products, review your content, take your call, book an appointment, answer your questions, hear your demo, consider your solution, champion your vision inside the organization—is a small win for you. Each progressive step makes you feel successful and boosts motivation so you will take the next step and the next step, until you reach your goal.

As a leader, you also must create small wins for your buyers and internal partners. They need to feel successful, too, and this motivates them to take the next steps toward your shared vision. Imagine what it's like for buyers like Kelly. She oversees learning and development for a North American shipping company. The inside sales team, based in eight locations, keeps expanding and now numbers nearly 250 agents. New hires often leave within six months, citing an inability to succeed because there's no sales training. Kelly doesn't have a sales background and doesn't have anyone on her team who could develop a sales training curriculum. She needs an external resource to help her develop and deliver on-boarding and selling skills training.

Kelly has been trying to get budget approval and move this project forward for two years. The problem keeps growing—seemingly constant hiring of new sales agents, continual turnover, disappointing sales numbers due to retention issues, frustrated sales managers, lost sales opportunities, and lots of pressure on her to get training in place. When Kelly finally received budget approval, it came with one key condition: gain consensus from all eight regional sales directors about the training vendor and program. Kelly was shocked that they did not immediately accept her recommendation to use the training company she'd selected after an exhaustive search and comparative analysis. She felt as though she was back at square one, with three of the sales directors lobbying hard for sales trainers they'd worked with before.

> **While buyers are reaching for great heights, you want them to feel excited by the possibilities, not fearful of failure.**

If you were the seller Kelly had originally selected, you'd want her to feel committed to you. You'd want her to feel motivated and inspired by the shared vision you'd created with her. You'd also want her to feel so strongly about doing business with you that she wouldn't cave in to the regional sales managers' demands, something she might be tempted to do just to start this project.

Your role as a leader is to prepare people like Kelly for moments like these. Along the way, small wins might have helped Kelly be a stronger internal champion and put this training program in place sooner. With coaching, she might have been able to win those regional directors over, one by one. With some sample tools from training, she might have been able to demonstrate early success with a pilot program. Booking a meeting for your training company to present to sales directors would also have been a small win, one that would have increased familiarity and top of mind awareness. These incremental successes would have empowered Kelly to proactively pursue change.

There's a delicate balance in play here. The shared vision between a buyer and a seller must be big enough to be exciting and ennobling. But it can't be so bold that it seems impossible and overwhelming. While buyers are reaching for great heights, you want them to feel excited by the possibilities, not fearful of failure. You must break the work down into small steps to make it something they want to be involved in and are committed to long term.

With any change, there will be hiccups, hardships, and setbacks. Leaders aren't able to eliminate all the struggles, but they are able to help people feel supported even as they are struggling. That's what Kelly needs in her current situation, a seller who will step in as a leader so she doesn't feel alone, unsupported, anxious, and frustrated.

Supporting others in challenging situations is easier to do when you have fortitude, stamina, and thick skin of your own. Psychologists have discovered that people who experience a high degree of stress and yet can cope with it in a positive manner have a distinctive attitude, one they call "psychological hardiness."[2] People with high psychological hardiness are much more likely to withstand serious challenges and bounce back from failure than those with low hardiness.[3] Hardiness is a quality people can learn and leaders can support.

Haley Katsman told us how she found herself in a situation that most sellers experience at some time in their careers. For Haley, it was when she was a field sales rep at a software startup. She juggled inbound leads, generated her own outbound leads, and closed deals. She saw opportunity with a mid-size technology company and had attempted to make inroads with numerous contacts in the organization. She hoped to generate interest and find an internal champion. After numerous emails, voice mails, and social connections, she finally received a response from a potential decision-maker. She opened the email with great anticipation, but it wasn't what she'd hoped to see.

I was immediately disheartened. It was such a brutal response. He began by telling me that he wasn't interested and critiqued each line of my email. I was first surprised, then irritated, and then angry. After staring at my computer screen for a few minutes, I took a deep breath and thought about how I would respond.

Instead of deleting his email or sending a rude response, I used this opportunity to try to build a relationship. I read his email again, without assuming bad intention. I considered his advice and sent a response that acknowledged each of his comments. I explained how we might be able to help him and his team based on the points from his email. I also put together a pitch deck, tailored to his team and company. It was definitely a long shot, but I figured it was worth a try.

You must remain open to the possibilities and look for ways to learn at every turn.

Haley demonstrated the three ingredients of psychological hardiness—*commitment, control,* and *challenge*—in responding to a setback. She turned adversity into advantage and committed herself to doing something about it. She took control of the situation, rather than letting it control her. She didn't sit back and wait. Instead of seeing the situation as a threat, she saw it as a new challenge. She seized the opportunity to learn and decided to try to make something happen, even though it was a long shot.

Before the day's end, I received a phone call from the prospect. I was shocked. His opening line was an apology for being so rude in his initial response. He proceeded to tell me that he was very impressed with my email and the pitch deck, plus the fact that he'd received a response at all. He wanted to set up a meeting to learn more about our platform. Fast forward three months later, and I received a signed contract from this same prospect. Some of my best wins come from unexpected or unusual scenarios.

As Haley's experience demonstrates, the ability to cope with disappointments and challenges depends on your mindset. To respond the way Haley did, you must believe you can influence the outcome. You must remain open to the possibilities and look for ways to learn at every turn. With a hardy attitude, you can transform stressful events into positive opportunities for growth and renewal. And you can help buyers feel the same way.

Haley's story has a happy ending. She turned the critical prospect into a satisfied customer. Her real win, though, came from her mindset when she wrote that response. She saw a way to reclaim something positive from the exchange, and she proved to herself that she was strong in standing proud.

LEARN FROM EXPERIENCE

Mindset matters.[4] If you believe you are powerless to effect change, you'll miss your opportunities to do so. Instead of learning from challenges and disappointments, you'll feel negatively about them. Negativity is contagious and repels buyers. When you fail, look for ways to

> Concealing mistakes plants seeds of doubt in the buyer's mind.

reframe your failures as learning and growth experiences.

You can formalize this process and conduct "lessons learned" reviews. With your buyers or internal partners, talk openly about what worked and what did not. Don't dwell on blame or shame for what didn't work. Instead, ask what you could do differently next time. Make it a priority to learn together anytime things don't go as expected. One buyer told us such "lessons learned" meetings with sellers were very important, a top priority. Another said, "It's good to work together as a team and to go over things—positive as well as negative—and to think about how we can better ourselves and the company in the future."

For some sellers, the idea of baring your failures and errors to buyers may seem strange. But consider these three very important truths:

☑ **Your Buyers Already Know Something Didn't Go as Planned or Promised.**

Concealing mistakes plants seeds of doubt in the buyer's mind. They may wonder if you're aware of the mistakes. If it appears you're not aware, they may feel apprehensive because now there's a good chance the mistakes could happen again. Buyers need to know you're in control when there are mistakes. You want your buyers to feel the way this one did after a problem occurred: "The product had an issue, and the seller was helpful with fixing it, by listening and being open and honest. The seller came up with solutions on how to prevent this from happening again. It made me feel great, less stressed, and more confident in the seller as a long-term partner."

☑ **When You Acknowledge Mistakes and Seize Opportunities to Learn from Failure, You Set a Standard for Your Buyers.**

Perhaps they won't let their fear of failure prevent them from taking risks to champion your shared vision when the going gets tough. You want your buyers to think of you the way this one thinks: "I have a vendor that often faces issues with their raw material suppliers. They always focus on our relationship first. Then they look for creative ways of overcoming the obstacle. It's all out in the open. I've learned a lot from their approach."

☑ **Being Vulnerable and Open Makes You More Trustworthy.**

In the buyer/seller relationship, trust is hard to build and easy to lose. Being transparent keeps buyers like this one happy: "There was a problem with an order I placed with the seller. They were on the ball communicating with us, no smoke and mirrors, and they did everything in their power to make sure we were happy. They gave us a discount for the mistake they made, and they were very professional. It made us have confidence in that company and trust in those sales people."

 The more that sellers agreed that they ask *"What can we learn when things don't go as expected?"* the more they reported feeling motivated and effective in meeting the demands of their jobs.

Failure is bound to happen at some point when you're pursuing possibilities and challenging the status quo. It's what you do in response to the failure that matters most. That's what experimentation is all about, and that's how you should think about it even before you begin. There's bound to be trial and error involved in testing new concepts, new methods, and new practices. Your buyers don't expect perfection. They expect effort to prevent problems as well as acknowledgment when failures or setbacks do occur. You can proactively set expectations on the front end, too, so no one is surprised when learning opportunities manifest.

There are opportunities for learning in everything you do. Learning is essential for leading. In

Learning is a master skill. In a rapidly changing world, it's also a survival skill.

fact, the best leaders are the best learners. A series of empirical studies sought to find out whether leaders learned differently from others; was there something special or unique about their learning styles?[5] The studies concluded that you could learn leadership in a variety of ways, and certain learning styles contribute to more effectiveness in some leadership practices than others do, but there is no one best style for learning everything there is to know about leadership. The style is not what led to achievement.

What turned out to be most important was the *extent* to which individuals engaged in whatever learning style worked for them. As you are learning to lead your buyers, dedicate time to learning. Throw yourself wholeheartedly into experimenting, reflecting, reading, or receiving coaching—do more of whatever learning approach works for you.

Learning is a master skill. In a rapidly changing world, it's also a survival skill. Your willingness and capability to learn from experience and to subsequently apply that learning to perform in different situations and circumstances will make you more successful.[6] This is the concept of *learning agility*. People who are highly agile learners continuously seek out new challenges, actively seek feedback from others to grow and develop, tend to self-reflect, and evaluate their experiences so they can draw practical conclusions.

When you demonstrate openness to learning and willingness to grow, you create a climate in which others can learn, too. As a leader, you'll have to model some vulnerability to let people know you're serious about learning. Ask your buyers for feedback about how you're doing. Learn from constructive criticism even though it stings to hear it. View the success of others as an inspiration and not as a threat. When you believe you can continuously learn, you will. Only those who believe they can get better make an effort to do so.

The climate for learning starts with what you model and grows when there is a high degree of trust. Without trust, people can't be vulnerable enough to admit when they don't know something or to ask for help. This is one reason why you must build trust before you openly challenge your buyers. When trust has been established, they'll understand your positive intentions whenever you challenge them. They can have a more open and honest dialogue in response to your challenging questions. Without trust, they'll assume your challenges are self-serving. They may become defensive and agitated. No one can learn when these unproductive assumptions and responses take over.

With a climate of learning, you can facilitate brainstorming and idea generation, along with discussion about how to improve and how to achieve your shared vision. You can make it fun to learn and dismantle some of your buyers' natural aversions to taking risks. The openness and experience of learning can contribute to the awesome connecting experience your buyers desire. Part of that experience, buyers told us, is how much they like it when sellers ask questions that make them pause and think. Buyers are busy, and they may not slow down to reflect on long-term vision and big-picture thinking. They may not set aside and dedicate time for learning. When you bring learning into their experience with you, you create value for the buyer that is relevant and timely.

The climate for learning starts with what you model and grows when there is a high degree of trust.

Persevering and believing deep down that you can make an impact will set you apart as a leader. Devoting yourself to continuous learning and growing will strengthen your will and your skill. You will overcome great odds, make progress, change the way things are, and achieve extraordinary sales results.

Take Action: Experiment and Take Risks

Leaders experiment and take risks by consistently generating small wins and learning from experience. This means you must:

1. Create opportunities for small wins, promoting meaningful progress.

2. Set incremental goals and milestones, breaking big projects down into achievable steps.

3. Make it safe for buyers and internal partners to experiment and take risks by debriefing successes and failures, capturing lessons learned, and promoting learning from experience.

4. Remain open to new information and perspectives, and emphasize how personal fulfillment results from continually challenging oneself to improve.

5. Continuously experiment with new ideas through market trials, pilot projects, A/B split testing, and proof of concept demonstrations.

ENABLE OTHERS TO ACT

Sales enablement is all the rage. It's a sweeping term that encompasses all the technology, systems, practices, processes, training, and tools that help sellers produce results faster. Buyer enablement is another matter; it's far less common and a concept many sales organizations resist, reject, or simply ignore. Sharing control of the sale with the buyer and trusting buyers to make informed decisions without sellers seems risky. But buyer enablement is critical to sales success.

Buyers desperately want to be involved in collaborative idea generation and decision making. B2B buyers in our study rated Enable Others to Act as the most essential of The Five Practices of Exemplary Leadership. For a majority of sellers, this comes as a surprise, because it's the one they ranked as least important: They don't see how this leadership practice relates to selling.

But leaders know they cannot do extraordinary things alone. That's why they invest in creating trustworthy relationships. They build spirited and cohesive teams, actively involving others in planning and providing sufficient latitude to make their own decisions. Leaders develop collaborative goals and cooperative relationships. They are attuned to the needs and interests of others. Leaders bring individuals together, creating an atmosphere in which people understand that they have a shared future. Leaders make sure that everyone wins; and that no one wins at the expense of another.

Mutual respect is what sustains extraordinary efforts and results. Leaders nurture self-esteem in others. They make people feel strong, capable, and confident to take both initiative and responsibility. They build the skills and abilities of their buyers and internal partners to deliver on commitments. They create a climate in which people feel in control of their own lives. One buyer described an exemplary seller as an individual who does all this: "A seller who can brainstorm to improve my business with my own ideas and make them come true is my choice every time." This buyer is describing an awesome connecting experience, one that occurs because the buyer is enabled to participate in creating what he or she wants.

As an exemplary seller, you engage in the leadership practice of *Enable Others to Act* when you

- **Foster collaboration by building trust and facilitating relationships.**
- **Strengthen others by increasing self-determination and developing competence.**

9 | FOSTER COLLABORATION

STEVE FORTIN, COO OF SIERRA CASCADE NURSERY (SCN), set out to repair and solidify his company's relationship with their largest customer, Driscoll's. The companies shared a commitment to producing the highest quality products using the most sustainable practices available. But they lacked alignment in how to achieve this common purpose. Steve Griffiths, nursery vice president for Driscoll's of the Americas, also wanted improvement in the relationships between SCN and Driscoll's team members. The past few years had been plagued with misunderstandings that resulted in costly business mistakes. Communication breakdowns and sloppy handoffs had compromised the level of quality each organization delivered.

Trust was at an all-time low. People were jumping to conclusions, misinterpreting email exchanges, withholding information, and assuming the worst. Past mistakes on both sides loomed large, fueling unfounded suspicions about underlying motives. Finger-pointing and unproductive negativity gripped both teams.

Both Steves agreed that persuading team members to work together was a top priority. Sierra Cascade, in the role of vendor, took the lead. The objectives for fostering collaboration, as outlined by Steve Fortin, included:

- ➤ Being more transparent and explaining what we're doing before we do it.
- ➤ Showing respect and stop reacting like victims when our customer makes strategic decisions we don't agree with.
- ➤ Understanding the impact of our decisions on our customer.
- ➤ Understanding the strategic plans of our customer so we can be supportive.
- ➤ Showing more humility and being more open to our customer's input and ideas.

Making these changes would take serious effort. They needed to address past mistakes and rebuild trust. They needed a new beginning. Steve and Steve convened twenty managers, representing key functional areas from both companies, for an intensive retreat. They started by eliminating any elephants in the room. To give everyone a voice, they conducted an anonymous survey as a safe way to vent frustrations and offer individual perspectives. The survey gave every team member an opportunity to express what it would take to rebuild trust and relationships.

Thanks to the survey and the modeling of collaboration from the top, the retreat started positively. People knew they'd been heard. They were able to listen to others more openly. They addressed hurt feelings, misunderstandings, and negative assumptions directly and respectfully. Team members asked each other why and how certain decisions had been made. They shared details about the impact of those decisions, and they explained what they'd prefer in the future. They left with an action plan to communicate new protocols, a partnership approach throughout both organizations, and commitments to collaborate and communicate more openly and more proactively.

Over the next twelve months, the teams showed steady improvement. Looking back, Steve Griffiths said:

*The conversations these past few months have been the best we've
ever had. Collaboration on some big projects has been outstanding.
People are more respectful. They seem to like each other again. Instead of talking all the time about problems, they're talking about
solutions. I never hear the same kinds of complaints about people
that I used to. That negative and divisive talk has really subsided.
Now we're doing more together. Sierra Cascade even sent a team to
Mexico to build some machinery for us there. Our trust is at an all-
time high. You can see it in our discussions about pricing and planning. Sure, we've still had challenges, but we've faced them well and
we've faced them together.*

As Steve and Steve demonstrated, creating a climate of trust and
facilitating relationships smoothes the road to success, even when the
conditions are challenging. Leaders know you can't do it all alone, and
they build their teams around a common purpose and with mutual
respect. Leaders make trust and teamwork high priorities.

> **The level of commitment that sellers report is directly
> related to the extent to which they develop cooperative
> relationships among the people they work with.**

Extraordinary performance isn't possible unless there's a strong
sense of shared creation and shared responsibility. Exemplary leaders
make the commitment to *Foster Collaboration* by engaging in these
essentials:

- **Create a climate of trust**
- **Facilitate relationships**

Collaboration between sellers and buyers is critical for achieving
and sustaining high performance. As more decision-makers become
involved in purchasing, you'll need skills to navigate conflicting interests and tensions that arise. Because buyers are demanding an

experience that allows them to be participants in creating what they want, you must focus on building trusting relationships, the very core of fostering collaboration.

CREATE A CLIMATE OF TRUST

More choices. More decision-makers. More complexity. More workload. More distractions. Getting through the purchasing cycle with a buyer has never been more difficult. The changes to buyer/seller dynamics require considerable collaboration from the moment a new relationship begins. Your winning strategies will be based on a "We, not I" approach.

There is no "we" without trust. It's central to human relationships. Without trust, you cannot lead. Without trust, you can't get buyers to believe in you or the message you bring. Without trust, you cannot accomplish extraordinary things. Sellers who are unable to trust others fail to become leaders. They end up doing too much of the work themselves or micromanaging every little detail. Their lack of trust in buyers and internal partners results in others' reciprocally lacking trust in them. To create an awesome connecting experience where buyers participate in creating what they want, you must trust them. Inside your organization, to unite team members you must first trust them.

For personal and professional reasons, sellers benefit from being more trusting. People who are trusting are more likely to be happy and psychologically adjusted than those who view the world with suspicion and distrust.[1] People perceived as trusting are sought out more as friends, are more frequently listened to, and are subsequently

> **Without trust, you cannot lead. Without trust, you can't get buyers to believe in you or the message you bring.**

more influential.[2] When you trust your buyers, they are more likely to trust you.

When they are weary from rejection, continuances, and objections, sellers may view buyers as opponents instead of allies. In these circumstances, your responses to buyers may inadvertently signal mistrust. Typical examples include:

- Gatekeepers say decision-makers are in meetings. Decision-makers say they're too busy to meet. Sellers don't believe what's reported and are discouraged by these barriers.

- Sellers want to get in front of the ultimate decision-maker. When they learn they've been presenting to an information gatherer or only part of a decision team, they feel deceived.

- Sellers seldom believe the budget limits given. They assume buyers give a low-ball number to anchor upcoming price negotiations.

- Objections are thought to be smoke screens to give the buyer leverage in negotiating a better deal.

- When buyers report disappointing results post-purchase, sellers are skeptical and think it's a strong-arm tactic to get something more.

A common theme in sales blog posts, speaker rants, and training is "buyers are liars." At the 2017 National Automobile Dealers Association annual convention, attending car sellers and dealers said the number one problem in their industry is dishonest buyers.[3] People buying cars seem to think the same of sellers, so the mutually negative perceptions cause both sides to be wary in all interactions. This sets sellers up to fail when it comes to creating a climate of trust. Starting with the belief that buyers are inherently untruthful is unfair and inaccurate. It's no truer or fairer than buyer perceptions that all sellers are greedy. Reflexive reactions on both sides interfere with trust building. The more a seller projects reservations, the more a buyer will respond in kind. It's up to the seller, as a leader, to be the first to trust.

You need to let down your guard and be vulnerable enough to take a chance with every buyer you encounter.

In our research, buyers told us they expect sellers to show them trust and respect when:

> ➤ **They Need Time to Make a Decision.** "Allow me time to research on my own without interference."

> ➤ **There's an Unexpected Change.** "The seller went above and beyond and called me at home to ensure we were on the same page. He didn't keep anything from me."

> ➤ **They Ask Questions.** "I do not like it when a seller talks over me or doesn't listen. I do like it very much when all my questions are answered in detail."

> ➤ **They Express an Opinion.** "I like when a seller is interested in what we do to make the company better. I want my seller to be a team player, to have confidence in me and my opinions, but also have his or her own opinion."

> ➤ **At All Times!** "I want the seller to always keep me involved in everything going on in the purchase."

Being the first to trust feels risky. You'll be taking a chance, making yourself vulnerable. But you'll never break through with a buyer until you establish trust, and the payoff could be huge.

To start, let buyers know what you stand for, what you value, what you want and hope for them, and what you're willing to do. These actions will differentiate you from other sellers who talk about products and services, not personal values and commitments. There's no guarantee buyers will respond immediately or understand your intentions. But once you take the risk of being open, buyers are more likely to take a similar risk—albeit tentatively—and work with you to develop mutual understanding.

It's up to the seller, as a leader, to be the first to trust.

People want to trust other people. Buyers proceed cautiously because of negative seller stereotypes. At the same time, they're looking
for evidence that they can trust you. One thing you can do is to demonstrate concern for the buyer. Showing concern is one of the clearest
and most unambiguous signals of trustworthiness. When others know
you'll put their interests ahead of your own, they won't be as hesitant
to trust you.[4] Listening, paying attention to buyers' ideas and concerns,
answering their questions fully, helping them solve their problems,
and being open to their input are simple yet powerful ways you can
demonstrate genuine interest and concern. Those words—*"genuine
interest"*—were used over and over again when we asked buyers what
they wanted to see more of from sellers.

Notice that listening leads the list of actions demonstrating genuine concern and interest. It, too, is a word buyers used frequently
in our study. Each action in the list above requires *quality listening*,
which means using more than your ears. Your brain must be engaged to focus, process, and comprehend what your buyer is saying.
You must also use your heart to listen for the feelings (not just the
content) in what's being shared. In an analysis of over 10,000 sales
calls, buyers noticed and favorably re-
sponded when sellers improved the
quality of their listening and the quality of the questions they asked.[5] The
sellers who listened best earned buyer
trust the fastest and advanced more
sales. Buyers in our research, too, com-
mented about the links between listening and trust:

> **You'll never break through with a buyer until you establish trust.**

> ➤ "Listening creates a personal relationship. The seller knows
>   about me and what's important to me."

> ➤ "A positive attitude and a willingness to listen helps me trust
>   them."

> ➤ "I am most willing to work with sellers who truly listen to my
>   needs."

Buyers associate quality listening with trustworthiness and respect. By listening for feelings, you can empathize and connect emotionally, which goes a long way in building trust.[6] When you listen well and show empathy, you're dignifying your buyer. Treating others with dignity and respect is critical, and sellers who fail to do so seldom have a second chance.

 The sellers who rated themselves the most productive indicated that they treat people with dignity and respect nearly three times more often than those who were at the bottom of the productivity scale.

There's another aspect of fostering collaboration that buyers expect from sellers. Of all the seller behaviors discussed in our study, this one ranked at the very top: *Buyers want sellers to share information and knowledge.* In other words, they want to be treated with respect, and you do this when you answer their questions immediately. They want information that is timely, relevant, and useful. They don't want sellers to withhold information.

Buyers' desire for immediate information presents a dilemma. Take, for example, the price question. Buyers are asking about cost sooner because they've done lots of research before talking with a seller. But sellers are trained not to divulge price until they establish value. When buyers ask for price early on, sellers deflect the question. Deflecting annoys buyers and makes them mistrustful. In a HubSpot Sales Perception Study, the differences between what buyers want to talk about and what sellers actually talk about were stark, as shown in Figure 9.1.[7] For example, in the first sales call, 58 percent of buyers want to discuss price, but only 23 percent of sellers are willing to do so.

Leaders don't withhold information. They know trusting others with information increases the likelihood that buyers will share information in return. Sellers who are mistrustful or unwilling to share erect barriers with buyers. Transparently sharing

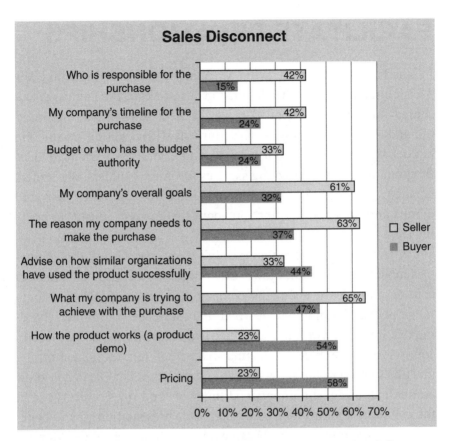

Figure 9.1. What Customers Want to Discuss in the First Sales Call vs. What Sales Reps Typically Cover

Source: Buyers Speak Out: How Sales Needs Evolve. HubSpot Sales Perception Study 2016. 505 Global Consumers/115 Global Sales Professionals. Used with Permission.

information—even sensitive information like pricing—builds trust and fosters collaboration.

Sharing information has a secondary benefit. People want to follow leaders who are competent. When you provide information that is relevant, timely, and useful, you look knowledgeable, capable, confident, and competent. Sharing gives you the opportunity to convey your insights and knowledge, to demonstrate lessons learned through experience, and to boost the buyer's confidence in you.

FACILITATE RELATIONSHIPS

Lemna Parker persevered. While working to get a meeting with a key decision-maker, she built relationships throughout the company. She shared information, extended trust, listened, showed genuine interest, and—slowly but surely—made inroads with a volume production builder she knew she could help. Lemna sold The Guaranteed Sales Program, a suite of marketing services for home builders. She called, emailed, and stopped by the corporate office frequently. She delivered donuts and provided information about the builder industry to break the ice.

When her usual techniques didn't work, she visited the company's model homes around town. Each time, she'd engage on-site sales counselors to learn about the company's business model and long-range plans. The more she learned, the more she could offer. Building relationships with the front office team at corporate and with sales counselors finally paid off. Lemna was invited to a Monday morning meeting to present her program to the sales team. Thanks to her information gathering, she understood the goals and roles of everyone in the company and how she could help. Her presentation was so beneficial and on-point that she became a regular attendee at the Monday meetings, now positioned as a partner who offered valuable industry updates and information.

Lemna created interdependence with her target buyer. She made herself an invaluable resource. She developed cooperative relationships throughout the organization, giving useful information and receiving insights in return. Her collaboration with so many members of the builder's team positioned her as someone they could trust. When she demonstrated that their goals were her goals, too, she gave them a sense that "we're all in this together" and the success of one depends on the success of the other.

Sellers often miss opportunities to do what Lemna did. If a seller views a buyer as anything other than a potential partner, there's little chance of forming a collaborative and interdependent relationship.

When sellers see themselves as hunters and their buyers as targets or prey, the relationship can only be transactional and guarded. If you label your buyers as suspects, prospects, leads, key accounts, or any other term that lumps like buyers together, you risk over-generalizing and not getting to the individual level necessary for forming enduring and trusting relationships. Complicating the matter is the movement to more sales enablement, AI and automation tools, and social media. None of these can replace human-to-human connections. The lure of shortcuts and their false sense of familiarity impedes the formation of genuine relationships.

Sellers often miss opportunities to create a sense of "we're all in this together."

The personal-best stories we collected abound with examples of sellers who took the first steps to promote joint effort. Buyers were impressed by sellers' commitment and willingness to show they had the buyers' interests at heart. When sellers invest in relationships, buyers do, too. Take, for example, what Dianna Geairn did to put her buyer's needs ahead of her own. She was selling an enterprise software solution and was about to close a deal with a Fortune 100 company. Most sellers would take whatever a buyer of this magnitude would throw their way. Not Dianna. She risked losing it all because she was unwilling to do something that might have been problematic for the buyer.

Their procurement team came back to me with a decision to buy, but also with a mandate to start with a pilot program at 10 percent of the proposed price. I knew this would never produce the results they needed, and that this would end up being completely unsatisfactory for them. I calmly took the deal off the table, and I said, "It's no problem if your company isn't ready to make the full investment. We know pilot programs rarely work because customers who use them are not all in. But we are, so when you feel like you're ready to make the full investment and enjoy the full benefits, I'll be here."

It took several days for them to respond. My manager offered to help me close and suggested we reconsider the pilot program. I advised patience, and it paid off. They came back and accepted all our terms for an enterprise launch at full price.

> **When sellers invest in relationships, buyers will too.**

Dianna's buyer saw the value of the product. More importantly, he saw the value of a collaborative relationship with Dianna. He understood that what they'd accomplish together, with her involvement, would be superior to what he would accomplish alone. Her story epitomizes the value-creating experience buyers yearn for. Buyers in our research told us they wanted:

☑ **To Be Entrusted with Information.**

"The rep explained it thoroughly and then left it up to me to make a decision on whether or not to switch to the new product. He answered all my questions, but he did not push me one way or the other. In the end, I felt I made the correct choice, and I appreciated the way the rep handled this."

☑ **To Be Heard and Taken Seriously When They Have Input.**

"The sales reps reconfirmed the main points of what they understood. Then I clarified a few things. They came back with an even better choice. I was glad they paid attention to what I said."

☑ **To Feel Important and Ennobled.**

"They made me feel like their top priority. I really felt like they gave me their full attention. I appreciated it, and it made me choose them over others who seemed like they could take or leave my business."

The stroke of a key or click of a mouse won't get the same relationship results as live-time conversations.

☑ **To Be Treated with Respect and Not Taken for Granted.**

"The person who sells me 3D printing supplies is always cordial, friendly, and respectful. He is always curious about how sales are going and what sort of projects we're working on. I value our relationship and choose to buy direct from him, even though it costs a little more than buying supplies online."

☑ **To Feel That a Seller "Has Their Back" in the Event of a Mishap.**

"We have one rep who always goes above and beyond. Recently, the accounting department at his company issued us bills that did not reflect the pricing in the verbal agreement we had. He took the issue right to the head of the company and got us the percentage he'd promised."

In all these examples, buyers felt valued by a seller. They appreciated the chance to be involved and supported. Giving buyers this feeling is easier when connections are made face-to-face, voice-to-voice, or via video conferencing. The stroke of a key or click of a mouse won't get the same relationship results as live-time conversations. There are limits to virtual trust. Direct interaction with another human being is a more reliable way of creating identification, increasing adaptability, and reducing misunderstandings.[8]

Take Action: Foster Collaboration

Exemplary sellers Foster Collaboration by *building trust and facilitating relationships.* This means you must:

1. Extend trust to others, even if they haven't already extended it to you.

2. Spend time getting to know your buyers and internal partners; finding out what makes them tick, and showing concern for the problems and aspirations your buyers have.

3. Listen, listen, and listen some more.

4. Structure projects so there's a common goal that requires cooperation, making sure people know how they are interdependent with one another.

5. Find ways to interact directly with people and increase the durability of relationships.

10 | STRENGTHEN OTHERS

SAMANTHA ASSEMBLES MADE-TO-ORDER DISHES at a Chipotle Mexican Grill. Diners direct every step as she prepares their food. First, they choose a format—burrito, taco, salad, or bowl? Flour or corn tortilla? Crispy or soft? Next the protein—tofu, steak, carnitas, chicken, chorizo, barbacoa, or sofritas? Or some combination? Then the starch and veggies—cilantro-lime brown rice or white rice? Black or pinto beans? Any fajita-style veggies with that? Next, the salsa— mild fresh tomato, or tomatillo red or green chili, or roasted chili-corn salsa, or some blend? Finally, the toppings—lettuce, cheese, sour cream, guacamole?

Every order is unique. Every buyer tells Samantha precisely how to make his or her meal perfect. A little less of this, a little more of that. The dish is completely custom built, with an infinite number of ways to mix-and-match twenty-five ingredients.

Choice and the ability to create exactly what they want contribute greatly to buyers' loyalty to Chipotle. Despite a series of food-borne illness outbreaks in 2008–2009 and again in 2015–2016, fifty-seven new restaurants opened in 2016, comparable-store sales rose 17.8 percent and overall revenue increased 28.1 percent in the first quarter of 2017, and the company launched plans for rapid expansion in Europe.[1] Other restaurant chains have successfully emulated the build-your-own model to give buyers similar control. Subway was the first, and Chipotle upped the game. Now dozens of rapidly growing chains have applied the assembly line concept to a variety of cuisines. Buyers flock to other types of businesses, too, to participate in creating what they want. Retailers like Sur La Table, American Girl, Bass Pro Shops, and many more offer interactive purchasing experiences for buyers.

Samantha told us something interesting about Chipotle: Buyers want the opportunity to custom-craft their food, but most accept the standard offerings without much customization. She hears a lot more orders that sound like "Burrito, carnitas, white rice, pinto beans, corn salsa" than "Burrito with a mix of carnitas and chicken, no rice, pinto beans, light on the fajita veggies, extra cheese, corn salsa, and a little of the green chili tomatillo, too, with some guacamole on the side."

Knowing this, Chipotle could make a well-reasoned business case for eliminating the assembly line and standardizing a fixed number of options. Most buyers would still get the product they want, and the quality of ingredients would be unchanged. Chipotle could trim costs by eliminating expeditor and line manager positions that keep the assembly line model working efficiently. But giving up the assembly line would mean taking away the experience and control they've given buyers.

Chipotle knows, as do exemplary leaders, that transferring power and decision-making authority makes people feel trusted, enabled, ennobled, and in control. They help people both feel and be more powerful and capable of making things happen on their own.

The more sellers report that they support the decisions that people make on their own, the stronger are their feelings that they are making a difference in what they do and are effective in meeting the demands of their job.

To be clear, buyers are not rejecting the importance of relationships with sellers. On the contrary, buyers in our study said they want to see sellers exhibiting higher frequency in all the leadership behaviors that build relationships. Buyers want to have relationships with sellers. It's the *nature* of the relationship that must be redefined. There are four qualities to a buyer/seller relationship that are necessary for it to align with buyers' desires for self-determination:

☑ **Equality.**

Buyers want sellers to interact with them as equals. A successful buyer/seller relationship is not a power play. "They made themselves a partner, not just a vendor," is how one buyer put it. You don't need to be submissive to the buyer. The old saying "the customer is always right" is not helpful to B2B buyers. Insincere flattery, sycophancy, or deferential behaviors don't help buyers either. However, you do need to work with them as peers in a mutually respectful interaction.

☑ **Dialogue.**

Buyers want sellers to be confident enough to engage with them in two-way dialogue. You must ask quality questions and listen to the responses buyers give. You need to listen to the questions buyers ask and respond with complete, candid, timely responses. You must ask the tough questions and answer the difficult questions, as well. You need to be informed. As one buyer told us, "The seller had all the info on hand. They answered my questions in person and through email almost immediately. They knew their products inside and out, showing me they were passionate about what they do, and that's what convinced me to do business with them."

☑ **Involvement in Decisions.**

You must be willing to join with your buyers and be invested in their success. They want to feel involved in the decisions that are made about the products and services they purchase. Involvement takes times and commitment. Buyers resist when they feel rushed. "Provide me with what I want and, as we work together, show how new or more features will help our company. Don't try selling me everything you've got before we even get started." Inform buyers and give them choices when changes or unexpected circumstances arise. Put yourself in your buyers' shoes and understand which decisions affect them and how.

☑ Co-Creation.

Buyers want sellers to co-create insights and solutions with them. Don't think buyers will appreciate the insights and solutions that you generate without their involvement. You need to allocate time for brainstorming ideas and crafting solutions with buyers. You must find ways to allow buyers to participate in creating what they want. Buyers want to put their own personal imprint on the solution. You must value buyers' perspectives and have confidence in their abilities to make decisions that will support the shared vision.

The relationship buyers want is inspirational and cemented by common goals and a shared vision.

How this all comes together is well summarized by this buyer's observation:

The ideal is when a seller promotes an innovative or cutting-edge product, doing their best to answer all the questions we have. Then they invite our input so they can make relevant adjustments based on our specific requirements. Sometimes this is achieved through brainstorming sessions where we give our input and, by the end of the meeting, our contributions are recognized and complimented. All this helps to build a strong relationship between our company and the seller that lasts for a long time.

Forming a relationship requires more than chitchat and pleasantries, as one buyer explained: "I'm not big on small talk. I appreciate and expect professionalism in a relationship." Instead, buyers want to feel empowered and on par with sellers who interact with them as equals.

The relationship buyers want is not superficial. It's inspirational and cemented by common goals and a shared vision.

An awesome connecting experience is not a one-way production. Too many sellers focus on performing for and presenting to a buyer. Exemplary sellers focus instead on the buyer's involvement. They understand that ownership and commitment drive people to take responsibility for results and outcomes. Research indicates that when people feel psychological ownership of the work they're doing, they're significantly more committed to the group and its shared purpose. They are intrinsically motivated, more willing to take personal risks and to make sacrifices when they feel a sense of ownership in the work they do.[2] Exemplary sellers create and leverage this sense of psychological ownership as they work with their buyers to make extraordinary things happen.

DEVELOP COMPETENCE AND CONFIDENCE

Nordstrom department stores was looking for a way to manage internal employee directories. Providing technology and security solutions is Morris Abell's specialty. As a major accounts manager at Imanami, Morris works with senior executives at Fortune 1000 companies to help them with identity and access management.

It took nearly eight months to put the deal together. What Nordstrom envisioned would require customized enhancements. Imanami would have to dedicate critical product development resources to creating the very specific displays and reports Nordstrom needed. Morris realized that there were some they couldn't currently meet, but before saying, "We can't do it," he asked what the underlying drivers were:

I wanted to understand their true needs, not just the end product they envisioned. I knew I'd have to justify any modifications I asked

> **Buyers rated Enable Others to Act at the very top of the leadership practices they wanted more of from sellers.**

for, so this information would help me do that. I had to ask a lot of questions and listen carefully to get a complete and clear picture of what they wanted to accomplish. Once I understood their security concerns and the functionality they were looking for, I was able to expand the conversation and get our team creatively engaged in meeting their actual needs.

Morris empowered Nordstrom by working hard to understand what they wanted. He also empowered his technical team by enlisting and coordinating their help in crafting a solution. With everyone involved, he kept the focus on desired outcomes. Throughout development, Morris made every effort to get the right people into the conversations about what could or could not be done. Imanami and Nordstrom team members collaborated and together conducted tests. While Morris kept a close eye on their progress, he turned decision making and brainstorming over to the technical teams. "The best thing I could do for them," Morris said, "was to give them control of the process." He wanted them to have full ownership in what they were building together.

Choice, latitude, and accountability fuel your buyer's sense of power and control. Feeling strong, capable, and confident causes buyers to feel more committed to the work they must do as you strive with them toward a shared vision. Enhancing buyers' self-determination is essential for engaging them as participants in creating what they want. There's something more your buyers need to move forward with you. To feel competent as they execute the choices required, buyers need the appropriate knowledge, skills, information, and resources. Without these elements, they'll feel overwhelmed and disabled. Even with the requisite skills and resources, there may be times when they lack the self-confidence to do what's necessary.

As a seller, you may not have given much thought to developing the competence and confidence of your buyers. You might assume that the product you sell is enough to inspire buyer confidence, especially if it solves a problem. It would be easy to dismiss the behaviors required to Enable Others to Act and focus on the other four leadership practices because they seem more akin to classic selling notions. That would be a mistake. Buyers rated Enable Others to Act at the very top of the leadership practices they wanted more of from sellers.

To understand why it's so important to buyers, consider what happens behind the scenes. After you meet with a buyer and develop a shared vision, the buyer's work has just begun. First, your buyer will need to convince others inside his or her organization about the choice. That may involve conflict, debates, tradeoffs, promises, and uncomfortable questions. Your buyer will need budget approval. If your buyer directly manages the budget, the choice to allocate a portion of it to your solution means foregoing some or all of something else. This means saying "no" to others who are advocating for those resources. It may mean severing ties with another vendor who also has a relationship and history with the company.

Once everyone is convinced and the budget has been approved, there's even more work to do. Your buyer must coordinate or delegate all process and procedural changes, staff training, alignment, setup, and systems. Your buyer will be inundated with questions, concerns, and pushback as the changes triggered by working with you begin to occur. Your buyer's decision will be scrutinized. All this requires your buyer to take risks, to dedicate time and energy to the change, and to disrupt other work.

Feeling strong, capable, and confident causes buyers to feel more committed to the work they must do.

No one makes those kinds of sacrifices unless they feel competent, confident, and committed. Exemplary sellers create the conditions for buyers to feel supported and enabled. They stay tuned-in to make sure their buyers are continuously resourced and prepared for the challenges they will face. They don't stop at getting the buyer excited about the possibilities. They stick with buyers to strengthen their capacity and resolve when the going gets tough. They set buyers up for success.

People can't do what they don't know how to do. When buyers are unable to answer questions about your solution or don't understand all that's involved, they may backtrack or delay further action. In times of change and uncertainty, people feel vulnerable, hesitant, or doubtful. To support your buyers while they're working to gain internal commitment, and later when implementation begins, enhance their self-determination and build their competence and confidence by doing these three things:

☑ Be Available.

Educate, explain, and answer questions for buyers when they embark on something new with you. Review important information, check on the progress of critical steps, and make sure your buyer never feels abandoned. Buyers want to participate and have shared ownership, but they need you to remain a resource to them. They want you to be committed to helping them thoroughly prepare for next steps. One buyer, in fact, told us that this is extremely important in the buyer/seller relationship:

> One of the most important things is that the seller explains things to me to the point where I absolutely understand what's going on.

☑ Be Responsive.

If a buyer expresses concerns or doubts, don't take them lightly. These confidence gaps could derail the sale. Listen closely to pick up subtle clues when your buyers don't fully understand something or aren't completely confident in their ability to bring the vision to life inside their organization. Simple support makes a difference, as this buyer explains:

One time a seller came up with a plan that I wasn't sure I could handle. She showed me how others were using it and took me through the steps needed to convince others that this was the way to go.

☑ Be Respectful.

Conduct a two-way dialogue between equals. Even as you remain available and responsive, continue allowing your buyers to participate in creating what they want so they'll have a sense of ownership. Show your buyers that you support their decisions and ideas. One buyer says:

It's important that I'm able to have a rational back-and-forth conversation with someone and that we respect and understand each other's capabilities, knowledge, and professional situations.

Strengthening others is an essential step in a psychological process that affects people's intrinsic need for self-determination. People have an internal need to influence outcomes and decisions that impact them so they can experience a sense of order and stability in their lives. By building up your buyers' beliefs in themselves, you are bolstering their inner strength to forge ahead into uncharted territory, to make tough choices, and to face opposition because they believe in the vision, their skills, and their decision-making abilities. A variety of studies document that having confidence and believing in your ability to handle the job, no matter how difficult, are essential to promoting and sustaining consistent effort.[3] By communicating to buyers that you believe they will be successful, you help them extend themselves and persevere through challenging circumstances.

> **Exemplary sellers create the conditions for buyers to feel supported and enabled.**

Think of yourself as a coach for your buyer. Studies demonstrate higher levels of competence, confidence, and performance from people receiving coaching.[4] Coaches guide people in moving from where they are to where they want to be. NextGen Healthcare's VP of sales training, James Muir, teaches sellers how to coach buyers and become "the catalyst that empowers them to reach their goals." James says, "Coaching customers toward improvement is a noble purpose. Accept the challenge. Be their coach and guide them through each little commitment it takes to achieve their goals. Show them the way. Encourage and challenge them to take action."[5]

Good coaches ask good questions. The benefits of asking questions include giving others room to think, as well as to frame issues from their perspective. Asking questions indicates an underlying trust in people's abilities by shifting accountability, and it has the benefit of creating almost immediate buy-in for a solution. (After all, it's their idea!) Moreover, asking questions puts sellers in a coaching position to continue guiding buyers through their decisions and beyond.

Sales trainer Jeffrey Lipsius contends that coaching is the way to help buyers make good decisions. Through coaching, he says, you give buyers confidence, choice, and clarity. Jeffrey suggests coaching as a way to help buyers overcome self-limiting beliefs, self-doubt, and a lack of self-awareness.[6]

When leaders coach, educate, enhance self-determination, and otherwise share power, they're demonstrating deep trust in and respect for buyers' abilities. People who feel capable of influencing outcomes will be more invested in the work required to reach those outcomes. As you enable your buyers to act, they will, in fact, be more likely to act. You need competent and confident buyers to execute on the shared vision.

Asking questions indicates an underlying trust in people's abilities by shifting accountability, and it has the benefit of creating almost immediate buy-in for a solution.

Take Action: Strengthen Others

Leaders Strengthen Others *by increasing self-determination and developing competence.* This requires you to:

1. Take actions that make your buyers and internal partners feel powerful and in control of their circumstances.

2. Provide opportunities for people to make choices about how they do their work.

3. Structure roles and responsibilities so that people have opportunities to use their judgment, thus developing both greater competence and self-confidence.

4. Demonstrate your confidence in the capabilities of your buyers and internal partners.

5. Ask more questions to stimulate thinking.

ENCOURAGE THE HEART

Saying "It's been a pleasure doing business with you" isn't enough to sustain a relationship and foster repeat business. Buyers want more from their sellers than some obligatory courtesy at the end of a transaction. To make extraordinary sales happen, exemplary sellers find opportunities to show their appreciation and convey how they value their buyers at every step of the journey. They don't wait until the sale closes to show gratitude. They don't wait for the successful implementation of their solution to celebrate together.

Inside their organizations, leaders share credit and express pride in the collective effort of their internal partners. In their buyers' organizations, sellers publicly tell positive stories to bolster their buyers' confidence and commitment. Leaders do more than make people feel like heroes; they provide clarity and consistency around expectations for all the parties involved. They begin with the end in mind, are open to and seek feedback along the way about how things are going, and use this information to keep relationships and projects on track.

Leaders also know that relationships are sustained when people enjoy the company of those with whom they work. They find creative ways to celebrate accomplishments with their buyers. They take time out to notice and rejoice in reaching a milestone. They look for opportunities to make buyers feel good about decisions they've made and the work they're doing to reach the shared vision.

Leaders are sustained by more than the results, too. Sure, the commission check and celebration that come with reaching or exceeding quota are nice. But leaders are encouraged even more by seeing the differences they make in their buyers' lives.

As an exemplary seller, you engage in the leadership practice of *Encourage the Heart* when you:

- **Recognize contributions by showing appreciation for individual excellence.**
- **Celebrate the values and victories by creating a spirit of community.**

11 | RECOGNIZE CONTRIBUTIONS

DENNIS NARCISO WAS NEW TO HIS JOB AS TIME WAR-NER'S MARKETING DIRECTOR. With ambitious market penetration goals in Kansas City, he was looking for a creative, high-impact way to attract new cable TV subscribers. Dennis was brainstorming with Leon Toon, his newspaper advertising sales rep, when the big idea started to take shape. What they imagined had never been done and would change newspaper advertising forever. It would take time, commitment, and a lot of mutual support. "There were two different machines we had to bring together if we wanted to make it happen," says Leon. "It wasn't easy, but we really wanted it."

What Leon and Dennis wanted was to place full-page advertisements on the front page of *The Kansas City Star*'s weekly TV listings section. At the time, ads did not appear on front pages. It was a violation of everything sacred in journalism. Leon knew it would be an uphill battle. He persevered, with encouragement from Dennis, because he adamantly believed their idea would solve several problems. The section was a reader favorite, but it hadn't been profitable in years. Having a weekly sponsor would help keep the TV listings section off the chopping block.

Months later, after some back-and-forth internal negotiations for both of them, they received conditional go-ahead approval. Leon and

Dennis had to come to terms on the program specifics and pricing, but both focused on creating a mutually beneficial solution. "We were negotiating hard on points to make the program fit into our respective processes," Leon said, "but with the same vision in mind." Putting their plans in place required both to navigate internal politics, make compromises, and remain flexible. It wasn't easy. Both had to represent their own constituents and protect the interests of their own companies. All the while, they offered each other encouragement and support in their frequent check-in meetings. The idea was fragile and only came to life because they continually recognized each other's efforts to push it forward.

As Dennis and Leon fought to make their vision a reality, they knew they had one another's backs. When they got pushback inside their own organizations, they relied on each other for pep talks. They reminded each other of what could be instead of allowing themselves to dwell on the hardships related to making it happen.

Working together, Leon and Dennis eventually found all the support and approvals needed. "We both got the satisfaction of creating something completely new," said Leon, "seeing it through to success." They readily agreed that what made them succeed was how much each of them felt his efforts, hard work, commitment, and persistence were recognized and appreciated by the other.

The sellers who most frequently make a point of expressing their confidence in people's abilities give themselves an effectiveness rating that is more than ten times higher than those sellers who report rarely doing this.

Like Leon and Dennis, exemplary leaders know how important it is to connect with the people around them and to appreciate the risks they're taking and the hard work they're doing. All exemplary leaders make the commitment to Recognize Contributions. They do it because people need encouragement to function at their best and to persevere over time when the hours are long, the work is hard, and the task is daunting. Reaching the finish line requires repeated energy and unwavering commitment. Emotional fuel is needed to renew and replenish people's spirits.

To *Recognize Contributions*, you must utilize these two essentials:

- **Expect the best**
- **Personalize recognition**

By putting these two essentials into practice, you uplift your buyers' spirits and arouse their internal drives. You stimulate their efforts to reach for higher levels of performance and to stay true to shared visions and values. You help buyers find the courage to do things they haven't done before.

EXPECT THE BEST

Leon and Dennis's story demonstrates what happens when exemplary sellers believe in their buyers and their internal partners. Belief in people's abilities is essential to making extraordinary things happen. Exemplary leaders elicit commitment and get results because they firmly believe in others' abilities, all working toward a shared vision, to achieve even the most challenging goals. That's because positive expectations profoundly influence others' aspirations. They also unconsciously influence how you behave toward them.

You broadcast your beliefs about people in ways you may not even be aware of. You telegraph signals that say to people either "I know you can do it" or "There's no way you'll ever be able to do that." You can't accomplish much unless you show buyers and internal partners—through your words and your deeds—that you are confident in their abilities and drive.

Here's what makes Leon's actions particularly noteworthy. Although he's had a long and highly successful sales career with many accomplishments, when asked to recall a personal best in selling, it's this experience of encouraging his buyer that sticks out for him. Why? Because, he told us, "It wasn't about getting a deal done. It was about something a lot more exciting, struggling side-by-side with someone who could see the vision with me and see it through to the end, too." Leon and Dennis haven't worked together in many years. Nevertheless, they both say that this shared struggle and mutual encouragement in the face of adversity formed an enduring relationship and created outcomes they are proud of to this day.

Exemplary leaders bring out the best in others. If potential exists in some person or situation, they always find a way to release it. These leaders improve outcomes, performance, and results because they care deeply about the people involved and have an abiding faith in their capabilities. Exemplary sellers nurture, support, and encourage their buyers and internal partners. They set high expectations for themselves and others.

Leaders' positive expectations aren't fluff.[1] Expecting the best is about much more than keeping a positive outlook and psyching others up. The expectations you hold as a leader provide the framework into which buyers and internal partners fit their realities. Your positive expectations shape the way you behave toward others and how they engage in their work.

As incremental steps toward the shared vision, goals provide clarity on how work will be divvied up between the buyer and the seller. What's more, goals give context to recognition. Leaders Encourage the Heart in the context of shared purpose and vision. When people are clear about what they're striving for and why, the recognition they receive is elevated and more meaningful because it's linked to the shared vision.

With clarity about the shared vision, your buyers can see the exciting possibilities for the future. Setting

> **Exemplary leaders bring out the best in others. If potential exists in some person or situation, they always find a way to release it.**

goals with buyers and internal partners focuses their attention on the shared values and standards. This keeps everyone on track. Goals enable people to choose the kinds of actions they need to take, to know when they are making progress, and to realize when they need to course-correct. Goals give people an added commitment to seeing things through from idea to execution.

Along with goals, buyers appreciate feedback and input. Studies reveal that peoples' motivation to perform a task only increases when they have a challenging goal *and* receive feedback on their progress.[2] Goals without feedback, or feedback without goals, have little effect on people's motivation and willingness to put discretionary effort into the task.

The feedback you offer can be positive, as described by this buyer: "When the seller praises us for doing a good job, that's what impacts me the most. I like for them to tell me 'good job' after I've done something good." It can also be constructive feedback, as this buyer explains: "It makes me feel more secure to have honesty. Don't just say what you think I want to hear. Tell me the truth. If we need to improve our processes, say so. I like a sales team that shows concerns and ensures alignment of our procedures, goals, and values." Either way, feedback is the center of any learning process. If you're not offering your buyers and internal partners feedback, you're not helping anyone to improve.

> **Goals give context to recognition.**

People need feedback. They need to know how they're doing, and sharing no news has the same negative impact as giving bad news. There are five specific areas you can evaluate and about which you can give your buyers and internal partners feedback:

☑ Process Improvements.

If things are running smoothly, say so. If something seems to be slowing down the workflow or interfering with progress, share your thoughts. Don't assume or take charge of things you don't know about. Just ask the questions or make the observations.

☑ Change Management.

You're asking your buyer to lead change inside his or her organization. Help craft the change message and anticipate the barriers to change. Check in and offer encouragement and suggestions during the process of making change.

☑ Communication.

Set expectations early. How often will you be checking in with each other? What's the preferred method of communication? Who should be kept informed or updated? As you continue working toward your shared vision, hold others accountable to the agreed standards for communication.

☑ Decision Making.

If your buyer is working as an internal champion or change agent, find out how the decisions are made. Coach and prepare your buyer to influence decisions. Offer feedback about the common elements of your vision and how to share that information. Learn about the decision criteria and encourage your buyer to align the shared vision with the criteria.

☑ Progress Toward Goals.

Each time you meet with a buyer, determine next steps and action items. Report back to each other about the progress you're making on interim goals and what you need from each other to continue moving forward. Be sure to offer praise and recognition for the milestones reached and for the small wins achieved.

Learning doesn't happen without feedback. When you give your buyers feedback, you are giving them a gift. In turn, they'll understand what works and what doesn't work in your interactions. You will also benefit from asking for and considering your buyers' feedback. It's the only way for you to know whether your buyers believe you are committed and whether you're executing properly. Feedback and guidance are vital to the growth and development of all leaders. It is uncomfortable to hear and difficult to ask for feedback, but the negative consequences of not knowing what needs to be corrected can be far more costly.

Openness to feedback, especially negative feedback, is characteristic of the best learners, and it's something all leaders need to cultivate. When you seek and respond to feedback from your buyers, you will differentiate yourself. You'll also be setting an example and making it easier in turn for them to hear your suggestions. An awesome connecting experience is more than fun and games. To authentically connect, sellers need to be vulnerable, imperfect, and open to change.

What are some areas about which your buyers can give you feedback? How about *communications*? Ask your buyers what you could do differently to make them feel you are keeping in touch, providing adequate information, and helping them feel knowledgeable about what's transpiring. What about *supportiveness and availability*? Ask whether there is anything more or different they need from you to feel equipped for doing their part to realize the shared vision. The *quality of your work* could be another dimension to check out. Ask whether the work product you're providing meets their needs. Could you provide it in a different format, for example? Find out about your *impact*? Ask how your actions are affecting your buyers' performance. Are there adjustments in your timing or behavior that would help your buyers be more effective? Finally, explore your level of *credibility*. Ask whether you're living up to your promises, delivering what's expected, and making buyers confident in working with you.

> **When you give your buyers feedback, you are giving them a gift. In turn, they'll understand what works and what doesn't work in your interactions.**

> **When you seek and respond to feedback from your buyers, you differentiate yourself, set an example, and make it easier for them to hear your suggestions.**

When sellers provide a clear sense of direction and make feedback two-way, they encourage buyers to reach inside and do their best. Information about goals and progress toward those goals strongly influences people's abilities to learn and achieve. This also applies to leaders.[3] Encouragement is more personal and positive than other forms of feedback, and it's more likely to accomplish something that other forms cannot: strengthening trust between sellers and buyers and their extended teams. Encouragement, in this regard, is the highest form of feedback.

PERSONALIZE RECOGNITION

The team at protocol 80, Inc, an inbound marketing agency, was enjoying their newest client. Her professional speaking and training business was vastly different from their usual manufacturing and construction clients. While providing their standard website design, search engine optimization, and content marketing services, this new business let them learn about an unfamiliar sector. Not only that, but the client was personable and engaging. She'd sent bottles of her favorite wine to their offices in Bradford, Pennsylvania, so they could share a little taste of California. As they were getting acquainted, she'd asked them the icebreaker question: "If you were a box of cereal, what would you be and why?" Then she followed up by sending them their selections—steel-cut oats for Ashley, Captain Crunch® (all crunch berries) for Josh, Frosted Flakes® for the other Josh, and Life® for Donny. The relationship was off to a good start.

The transition from one digital agency to another is never easy. This one, though, was more complex than usual. The buyer was very active on social media, prolific in her content creation, and needing start-from-scratch inbound marketing strategies. Developing buyer personas, building website pop-ups and calls to action, and creating pathways to draw in new customers would take some time. The P80 team appreciated the buyer's patience and recognized that it was a steep learning curve for her. They wanted to express their appreciation to her in a way that would be impactful and have meaning.

In their online research about the client, they discovered that she was a rabid fan of The Kansas City Royals baseball team. She posted on Facebook about going to games. She wrote a series of blog posts about team leadership following their back-to-back trips to the World Series. Josh and Ashley also noticed posts about her "lucky" number thirty-three. With those two pieces of information, they picked a gift—a Royals jersey with her name and lucky number. It was perfect, just as they'd hoped. She told them it was, hands down, the "most thoughtful gift I've ever received from any business associate." When baseball season opened, she proudly wore the jersey and told anyone who'd listen how pleased she was with the personal attention and service P80 provided.

The P80 team created an emotionally positive experience for their buyer. By personalizing how they showed their appreciation, they made a lasting positive impact. A bouquet of flowers, though nice, simply wouldn't have had the same depth of meaning.

One of the most common complaints about recognition in the workplace is that it's highly predictable and impersonal. A one-size-fits-all approach to recognition feels insincere, forced, and thoughtless. Generalized statements of praise and recognition fail to be uplifting and encouraging because, without specifics, they seem obligatory or ingratiating. Making the extra effort to personalize recognition makes it far more meaningful to the recipient. At Yum! Brands, the world's largest restaurant company by units, every recognition award must be *personal* and carry a *handwritten* message.[4] The former CEO of Yum! Brands, David Novak, says the key to recognition is to make it personal to the person you're recognizing. He says, "Recognition is truly universal, and everyone, everywhere loves to be recognized for who he is and what he does well."[5]

When recognition is personal, it's more special. You get more emotional bang for your buck, whether it's with your buyers or internal partners. That's why it's so important for sellers to pay attention to the likes and dislikes of each individual. When you take the time to get to know people, you can recognize them in a way that they personally value because it's relevant to who they are and what they care about. In your quest to create an awesome connecting experience, personalized recognition is a powerful tool.

Sellers may not fully understand the need to recognize their buyers' contributions. When we presented this idea in a recent workshop, several sellers chimed in: "The buyer should be thanking *me*. I'm the one who solved a problem and helped them, not the other way around." This transactional way of looking at the exchange is over-simplified and short-sighted. No matter how smooth or easy the transaction was, the buyer did work that is well worth a seller's gratitude and recognition.

What's more, there's a secondary benefit to recognizing buyers. Whatever you praise or appreciate is more likely to be replicated; you are influencing future behavior. If a buyer is making decisions you like, taking actions you want to support, or otherwise behaving in ways that move you closer to your shared vision, then you will want to see more of those actions. Recognizing them increases your chances of seeing more of the same. Similarly, when an internal partner contributes to reaching shared goals, publicly recognizing the individual will signal for others what you appreciate and find worthy of praise. Then they can replicate those desirable behaviors, too.

Leaders make time to get acquainted with people so they can personalize recognition. Feeling a connection with a leader motivates people to work harder for the simple reason that people don't like to disappoint individuals they have a relationship with and care about. People are more willing to follow someone they feel knows who they are and what they need.

To make sure that your recognition is personal, be creative and have some fun. Don't be a broken record, praising your buyers and internal partners the same way over and over again. Acknowledge people for their contributions in creative ways. Don't make assumptions about what people like. For example, a gift card to a coffee shop might be exactly right for one buyer and absolutely wrong for another, depending on their individual preferences.

> **Whatever you praise or appreciate is more likely to be replicated.**

The way you recognize buyers need not be elaborate or expensive. In fact, many buyer organizations specifically forbid accepting gifts from vendors. In this case, getting creative may require a little more thought and imagination. Consider how you can give your buyer a low-cost or no-cost token of appreciation. The truth is that people respond to all kinds of informal recognition. Make your token of appreciation silly, like a Superman or Wonder Woman figurine to represent a heroic act in overcoming a tough challenge. Make it heartfelt, like a handmade card or handwritten note. Bake cookies, take photos of milestone celebrations; be imaginative in capturing meaningful moments for your buyers.

You don't need to include anything tangible. Genuine recognition will be heard and felt when you simply say "thank you" and give specifics about what you appreciate. Exemplary leaders make extensive use of intrinsic rewards. These are the rewards that are built right into the work itself, including factors like a sense of accomplishment, a chance to be creative, or the challenge of the work. All are tied directly to individual effort. This is why setting goals and checking in frequently are so important.

It all boils down to being thoughtful. The techniques you use are less important than your authenticity. Buyers in our survey repeatedly told us they want to work with sellers who have their best interests at heart. When you show that your care and concern are genuine, you demonstrate that you do, indeed, have the buyer's best interests in mind, not just the sale and your commission. When buyers believe you sincerely care, you become more than just another seller.

The simple, inexpensive, powerful, two-word phrase "thank you" can't be over-used. As long as your "thank you's" are genuine, they'll help buyers feel better about the work they're doing and the effort they're expending. Extraordinary achievements bloom more readily in climates marked with a high volume of appreciative comments. Buyers in our study were starved for appreciation from sellers, repeatedly pointing out that they just wanted sellers to say "thank you" once in a while. "It means the world to me," one buyer told us, "when a seller just gives an observation of the job that has been done" because "a lot of sellers don't even do that." Buyers feel taken for granted if there is no acknowledgment of the work they've done behind the scenes. As one buyer put it, "It is important for sellers to treat us appreciatively. I like to work with people who frequently encourage members of the project team who are striving the hardest to finish the project well."

Buyers want to work with a seller who has their best interests at heart. This is one way that buyers differentiate between sellers.

Thanking, recognizing, and encouraging your buyers isn't hard to do. The costs need not be exorbitant, and the gestures need not be lavish. Genuine praise and appreciation will solidify relationships with buyers, demonstrate your commitment and care, and pay huge dividends.

Take Action: Recognize Contributions

Exemplary leaders and sellers recognize contributions by *showing appreciation for individual excellence.* This requires you to:

1. Maintain high expectations about what you can accomplish as a team.

2. Communicate your positive expectations clearly and regularly.

3. Create an environment that makes it comfortable to receive and give personalized feedback.

4. Show imagination when it comes to recognition. Be spontaneous and have fun.

5. Make saying "thank you" a natural part of your everyday behavior.

12 | CELEBRATE THE VALUES AND VICTORIES

"WE GOT THE APPOINTMENT. NOW WHAT?" Phil Gerbyshak had secured a demo, but there was only one person inside the buyer organization excited about it. His team was disheartened by the lackluster reception they'd received as they gathered details to create a personalized demo. Without any pre-meetings, there was no opportunity to break the ice or get acquainted with the needs of decision-makers. Most team members felt they were wasting their time with the demo. Without the information they needed, they weren't sure they could conduct a successful demo of the brand-new product. Many were concerned about the product's functionality outside of the test environment. Phil was asking himself how to turn the situation around.

Phil realized they wouldn't be successful if his team was discouraged. He reminded each member of the team that this was a tremendous opportunity to learn and challenge themselves. He emphasized how they could use this demo as a soft launch, figuring out all the bugs in their presentation and process. He encouraged them to give it their all so they'd represent their brand positively and leave the demo smarter than they were before. He reduced their stress by taking the focus off making the sale. In doing so, he unified the group around their core values. Consequently, going in, they felt a strong sense of pride about their bravery and willingness to step outside their collective comfort zone.

Phil had something else working in his favor. This situation was going to be arduous and demanding, leaving little time for fun and celebration along the way. But Phil's team knew that would come eventually. His history of celebrating included events like an African Safari themed event, complete with stilt walkers, torches to light the way, with significant others included because they, too, were appreciated.

Phil also worked before and during the demo to encourage the lone internal champion in the buyer's organization. He helped her see the advantages of being an early adopter. He let her in on the secret that this was going to be a learning opportunity for everyone, and he made it sound like an adventure they were going to enjoy, no matter what happened. After Phil's initial reframing, his team did their best to be encouragers, too, by calling other stakeholders in the organization to get their buy-in.

Everyone on Phil's team was pleasantly surprised when the buyer approved a small pilot program, led by their original champion, who was now a true believer. Phil didn't want to lose her enthusiasm for the project, so he made a point to connect with her every single day for the next two months as they prepared for the pilot. Before the launch, the buyer surprised the team again, asking them if they could expand the pilot to five times its original size!

Once again, the team was concerned. Team members didn't know whether they could make it work. This time, however, they encouraged each other. Phil was proud to hear echoes of his own words about learning and growth opportunities, about thinking of the pilot as a soft launch, and how they had to start somewhere, sometime.

As they persevered, their buyer began to reciprocate all the encouragement and praise they'd heaped on her at the onset. She even flew in just to have lunch with the technical teams from both organizations and encourage everyone to keep trying. "It was the encouragement and teamwork that made us keep going," Phil told us. "We celebrated in little ways, whenever we could make the time to insert even a few moments of fun, like having our sales engineer demonstrate how fast he could solve a Rubik's Cube."

The constant encouragement we all gave each other to keep pressing forward made us stronger. We felt we were all in together, that one person's success was everyone's success. We celebrated when we made progress, and we dug deeper when we encountered a roadblock. We went from almost backing out to making a small start to making a big finish. I was incredibly proud of us.

Exemplary leaders know, as Phil did, that human beings are social animals, hardwired to connect with others.[1] People are meant to do things together, to form communities, and in this way to demonstrate a common bond. When social connections are strong and numerous, there's more trust, reciprocity, information flow, collective action, and happiness.[2]

Ninety percent of sellers who report that they very frequently find ways to celebrate accomplishments indicate a strong degree of team spirit versus only 30 percent of those who rarely celebrate.

Sellers are the conduits for connections between people in their organizations and their buyers' organizations. It's up to sellers to facilitate introductions and connections for those who will fulfill orders, provide customer service and support, and engage with buyers. Those can be button-down, all-business-all-the-time connections. Or they can be established, right from the start, as communities in which everyone has an understanding of the shared vision and commitment to common values. A feeling of community in the workplace infuses passion and purpose into the work, bonding people together, kindling hope in tough times, and enabling celebrations for all to share in when things go well.[3]

To strengthen this kind of connectedness exemplary leaders make a commitment to *Celebrate the Values and Victories* by mastering these essentials:

- **Create a spirit of community**
- **Be personally involved**

When you bring people together, rejoice in collective successes, and directly display your gratitude, you reinforce the essence of community. Being personally involved makes it clear that everyone is committed to making extraordinary things happen.

CREATE A SPIRIT OF COMMUNITY

Most sellers don't see the need for encouraging the hearts of buyers. Those who talk about this leadership practice at all often characterize it as more of an afterthought. They don't see that these behaviors are essential to the buyer/seller relationship, especially a durable one. They don't see how doing these things will increase their revenue production. When asked how they believe buyers ranked Encourage the Heart, most sellers thought they would put it at or near the bottom, assuming the other leadership practices are more important and valued by buyers.

But buyers feel quite differently. More than 96 percent of the B2B buyers in our study ranked Encourage the Heart over Challenge the Process and Inspire a Shared Vision. Buyers under thirty years old rated Encourage the Heart even higher, putting it second only to Enable Others to Act. Some buyers even select sellers with this specific leadership practice in mind, saying, "I ask for examples of how they have previously recognized some of their co-workers' accomplishments." Another buyer gave an example of a time when a seller creatively recognized her contributions to their shared success: "One seller donated materials to my outreach program. It was such a beautiful thing to do."

Sellers we've spoken to don't initially grasp why it's so important to celebrate with their buyers and internal partners. Many believe that the benefits of the products or services they've sold ought to be ample reward for the effort. Others suggest that sellers celebrate the sale (cha-ching!) and, separately, buyers should celebrate the problem solved.

The point these sellers are missing is that celebrations are a great way to encourage everyone and to bring the group together. Celebrations connect everyday actions and events to the common values and accomplishments of the team. They don't have to be elaborate. The simple acts, like donating to a buyer's philanthropic cause or hosting a lunch to encourage a struggling team, are what buyers remember.

Celebrations have a dual purpose. The first is to encourage people and uplift them emotionally so they can find the resolve and strength to continue forward. The word "encourage" literally means "to put courage in," and you can visualize it as pouring courage into the buyer's heart, replenishing the wellspring of emotional connection to the work and to you.

The second purpose of encouragement is to remind people who they are, what they've committed to, and how they should act in service of that commitment. Celebrations provide the perfect opportunity to explicitly communicate and reinforce the actions and behaviors that are important in realizing shared values and common goals. They provide a way to do both things at once—to encourage and to reinforce—with your buyers and internal partners.

In Chapter Eleven, we talked about individual recognition and how it increases a buyer's sense of personal worth and deepens commitment to the shared vision. Public celebrations do this, too, and they add other lasting benefits that private, individual recognition can't accomplish. For example, public events give you a chance to highlight examples of what it looks like for others to contribute effectively to the group's vision and values. When you shine the spotlight on buyers and internal partners, they become role models. They visibly represent how you would like others to behave, and they concretely prove that it's possible to do so. Public celebrations of accomplishment also build commitment, among both the individuals

> **Celebrations connect everyday actions and events to the common values and accomplishments of the team.**

recognized as well as all who are watching. When you communicate to individuals, "Keep up the good work; it's appreciated," you're saying to the larger group, "Here are people just like you who are examples of what we stand for and believe in. You can do this. You, too, can make a significant contribution to our success."

By singling out one person and recognizing him or her privately, you miss an opportunity to show others how you'd like each member of the team to work. Recognition that's done behind closed doors limits your effectiveness overall, making you too dependent on a single resource.

Private recognition also robs the team of shared celebration and its ability to elevate the workplace mood. Researchers have shown that people tend to pick up on the feelings and attitudes of those around them. This "emotional contagion" is often not realized consciously.[4] Circuits in the brain are activated when people see others act in a certain way; it's as if they had taken action themselves. Watching someone else can impact the brain in ways that mirror experiencing it directly.[5]

Celebrations communicate and reinforce the actions and behaviors that are important in realizing shared values and common goals.

Celebrating together also helps people to get know each other as people, not just as job functions. Exemplary sellers appreciate the benefits of forming friendships with internal partners and buyers. Studies prove substantive differences between the task performances of groups of friends versus acquaintances. In groups composed of acquaintances, individuals prefer to work alone and speak with other folks in the group only when necessary. Consequently, they are reluctant to seek help or let others know that mistakes are being made. Groups made up of friends, on the other hand, talk with one another right from the start of a project. They evaluate ideas more critically, give timely feedback when others are veering off course, and offer each other positive encouragement every step of the way.[6] Feeling a sense of connection with your buyers and internal partners fosters greater accountability, engagement, and commitment.

Buyers in our study affirmed the importance of forming friendships, not just relationships, with sellers. They told us about sellers who join them for holiday meals, how trust grows when they socialize outside the office, and what it means to them when a seller makes extra efforts to do more than "just a vendor" would do. Buyers who offered these comments linked them to the business benefit—feeling more confident with the seller, being more committed to outcomes, and being more willing to try new things. This kind of social support is vital to outstanding performance.

It's perfectly okay to have some fun, too. People just feel better about the work they're doing when they enjoy the people they're working with.[7] Research demonstrates that having fun enhances people's problem-solving skills, making them more creative and pro-

> **Exemplary sellers appreciate the benefits of forming friendships with internal partners and buyers.**

ductive. Another benefit, according to this buyer, is "if your team is enjoying the work they are doing and feel recognized for their hard work, they are more likely to go the extra mile when you need it the most."

Fun is practically guaranteed in celebrations, but sellers can't have fun with buyers if they're too inhibited. When sellers see themselves in a subservient role, they tend to make all meetings as brief and as professional as possible. They don't allow time for fun, and they suppress their natural personalities. Buyers want more. They want sellers to be authentic and to engage with them to create an awesome connecting experience. Let your guard down and have a little fun. Celebrate in a manner that expresses your authentic self, but make it a point to celebrate the values and victories you share with your buyers.

BE PERSONALLY INVOLVED

You can't lead from an ivory tower or sitting behind your computer screen. To be effective, leaders get involved. That's what First Data Business consultant Maxwell Bogner does with his prospects and accounts. He gets deeply involved. Max's book of business has been built largely on referrals. His clients are happy to refer him to others because he does things differently:

> With each new client, I do my best to be helpful and consultative in all things, not only my product. This mentality of caring first and selling second leads to referrals from clients and strong strategic partnerships. I strengthen my relationships with my partners by fully buying into their company culture. It's not uncommon for guests of businesses I work with to mistake me for one of the company's employees. What makes me effective in selling, I'm told, is that I am genuinely concerned for the well-being of everyone involved.

People don't care how much you know until they know how much you care for them.

Max's sales philosophy is unflappable. He makes a solid first impression with buyers, and he commits to becoming more deeply involved over time. He personally recognizes individuals along the way, and he celebrates successes with the group. His attention to company culture helps him to understand the values and vision of his clients, and he works to find alignment and build from there.

Our discussion of exemplary leadership began with Model the Way, and we've come full circle. Like Max, if you want others to believe in something, you have to be clear about your values and make sure your actions reflect what you believe. You have to set the example by being personally involved, not invisible or scarcely present.

You have to practice what you preach and be personally involved in celebrating the actions of others that contribute to your shared successes. As Max pointed out, it begins by genuinely caring about your buyers.

People don't care how much you know until they know how much you care for them. Sellers often enter into relationships with buyers from a deficit position. Buyers are conditioned to be skeptical about sellers' motives and trustworthiness. This pervasive negative stereotype haunts sellers everywhere: buyers don't believe you care about them at all, only about reaching into their wallet. Showing you care is critical. If you don't swiftly eradicate the misperception about you, it will be a barrier to forming a relationship with the buyer. You have to prove that you have your buyer's best interests at heart and that you genuinely care.

Simple gestures show you care, even from the very beginning of a new relationship. One buyer said all it takes initially is "greeting me warmly, being kind, and smiling." Others believe it takes "being very responsive" or "being respectful and nice" or "keeping promises." As the relationship progresses, buyers seem to measure seller caring by the extent they are listening, empathizing, collaborating, asking questions, sharing a vision, and being encouraging.

Not one single buyer in our study mentioned behaviors that are difficult to learn or require any sort of special skill. The evidence of caring is something you are capable of demonstrating. It's important to put that evidence out there for buyers to see plainly. Don't conceal your caring to appear businesslike or uber-professional. Your care for the buyer is what opens the door.

Buyers measure seller caring by the extent they are listening, empathizing, collaborating, asking questions, sharing a vision, and being encouraging.

People who perceive their colleagues as caring, research shows, are most likely to be sought out for advice and to be seen as a leader, and this, in turn, results in higher performance levels.[8] On the other hand, people indicate that when they feel they're being treated uncaringly at work, their response is to deliberately decrease their effort and lower the quality of their work.[9] To show your buyers you care, increase the frequency with which you:

➤ Talk about business needs that are not directly related to the product you sell. Seek to understand more about the business as a whole and the buyer as a person.

➤ Ask quality questions to stay current and aligned with your buyer's evolving needs. As you ask questions, stay fully present to listen actively and empathetically.

➤ Create ways that your buyers can participate in fashioning what they want. Brainstorm for new ideas and give your buyers a way to put their own imprint on solutions.

➤ Connect in a way that bolsters your buyers' courage for the challenges ahead. Provide your buyers with recognition and promote celebrations.

➤ Push back when you see a mistake or a blind spot. Once you've earned your buyer's trust, don't lose it by wimping out when candid conversations are needed.

Exemplary sellers also show they care about buyers and internal partners by getting personally involved in celebrating big accomplishments as well as recognizing small wins along the way. They know that this gives them opportunities to find as well as convey stories that put a human face on values.

First-person examples are always more compelling than third-party ones. It's that critical difference between "I saw it for myself" and "Someone told me about it." You need to be continually on the lookout for what your buyers and internal partners are doing well. That way, you can let the person or team know to keep up the excellent work. You can also tell others all about what you observed. You can give an eyewitness account of what it looks like to put shared values into practice. By recognizing a behavior in the context of the values represented, you bring the values to life for everyone else. Through the stories you tell, you dramatically and memorably illustrate how you expect people to act and to make decisions.

After studying professionals in life-and-death situations, cognitive psychologist Gary Klein concludes that stories are the most powerful method for both eliciting and disseminating knowledge.[10] The reason stories are so effective is that they are, by their very nature, public forms of communication. Storytelling is how people pass lessons from one generation to the next, culture to culture. Stories belong in every celebration and act of recognition to convey explicitly examples of excellence you'd like to see replicated.

Leaders who tell stories of encouragement about the good work of others make people feel personally valued. Buyers appreciate being the central figures in the stories you tell. One buyer shared a story about a seller who:

> *Always tells us stories about how amazing it is that we can outsell larger stores on her product. This boosts our morale and does wonders for job performance.*

When you're telling stories, you're *teaching* your buyers and internal partners. You're also motivating them to dig deeper and mobilizing them to take action. Bullet points on a PowerPoint slide will never be as effective as your stories about real people. Well-told stories reach people's emotions and deepen their commitment to the shared vision.

Through the stories you tell, you dramatically and memorably illustrate how you expect people to act and make decisions.

Exemplary sellers look for reasons to celebrate and gather stories every day. They become personally involved in recognizing, celebrating, and sharing stories with buyers and their internal partners. They use these opportunities to show they genuinely care, that they're paying attention, and that they notice when people contribute to the progress being made toward the shared vision.

Telling stories of encouragement about the good work of others makes people feel personally valued.

There will never be a shortage of opportunities to join together with your buyer to celebrate your shared values and victories. In good times or bad, gathering together to acknowledge those who have contributed and the actions that have led to success signals to everyone that their efforts made a difference. Their energy, enthusiasm, and well-being—and yours—will be the better for it.

Take Action: Celebrate the Values and the Victories

Exemplary leaders Celebrate the Values and Victories by *creating a spirit of community.* This means you must:

1. Take actions that demonstrate that you "have people's backs" and ensure they feel "part of the whole."

2. Put celebrations on the calendar, and make fun a fixture in your work environment—laugh and enjoy yourself, along with your buyers and internal partners.

3. Get personally involved in as many recognitions and celebrations as possible. Show you care by being visible to your buyers, especially in the tough times.

4. Never pass up an opportunity to share true stories about how people on your team—including your buyers—went above and beyond the call of duty.

5. Be sure to link victories with shared values and vision; that's why they matter.

13 | LEADERSHIP IS EVERYONE'S BUSINESS

THROUGHOUT THIS BOOK, WE'VE SHARED observations and stories from sellers who've made extraordinary things happen. They sell a wide variety of products and services, and they represent all age groups and experience levels. They work for companies of all sizes. These are professionals, sellers who regularly call on buyers and diligently work to reach their quotas. They experience their fair share of sales successes and inevitable sales slumps. The people we've written about, however, are regular people, just like you. Like leaders, they've made behavioral choices which allowed them to accomplish extraordinary things.

The stories came directly from sellers who described their personal bests in selling. Every story ended with a victory for the seller and a success for the buyer, too. The outcomes are impressive, but we didn't tell these stories merely because of those sales results. Rather, we focused on *how* sellers made extraordinary things happen. We identified the behaviors and actions that led to the successful outcomes. Exemplary sellers are those who exhibit these behaviors more frequently and, subsequently, are more welcomed by buyers. Sellers who lead are leaders who sell.

Being a leader doesn't mean you have a position of formal authority, a certain title, or a specific spot on an organizational chart. Leadership isn't for a chosen few. Leadership is about relationships, credibility, passion, and conviction, and, ultimately, about what you *do*.

You don't have to *look up* for leadership. You don't have to *look out* for leadership. You only have to *look inward*. You have the potential to lead your buyers and internal partners to places they have never been. But before you can lead others, you have to believe you can have a positive impact. Just as the best sellers are the ones who not only believe in what they sell and make use of it themselves, the first person you have to sell is yourself. You have to believe that your values are worthy and that what you do matters. You have to believe your words can inspire and your actions can move others. You have to have the confidence that you can comfortably engage in The Five Practices of Exemplary Leadership.

> **Sellers who lead are leaders who sell.**

At this very moment, you already have the capacity to lead. You already have buyers who want you to lead. The question is: What are you going to do to stop selling and start leading?

The buyers in our study left little room for doubt. They already are choosing sellers who exhibit leadership behaviors over sellers who do not. What's more, they say the ideal frequency of leadership behaviors is even higher than what they're seeing from the sellers with whom they've chosen to work. There's plenty of room for upping your game, and buyers will respond favorably to leadership behaviors that create an awesome connecting experience for them.

Leadership makes a difference. The best leaders bring out the best in others. Leadership has an impact on people's commitment, their willingness to put forth additional discretionary effort, to take personal initiative and responsibility, and to perform beyond the ordinary. You can have this effect on your buyers, giving them the courage to persevere when they meet challenges and must work inside their organizations to champion the shared vision. When you show up as a leader with your buyers, you help them to be strong leaders in their own right so others can follow them, too.

We're confident that you want to become the best leader you can be—and not just for your sake, not just to make more sales, but for the sake of your buyers and others in your shared pursuits. After all, it's unlikely you'd be reading this book if you didn't have this aspiration. The only remaining question is: How can you learn to lead?

At this very moment, you already have the capacity to lead. You already have buyers who want you to lead.

Learning leadership takes practice. It also takes practice to set aside the sales behaviors you've seen modeled by others and many of the sales habits you've acquired. The good news is that leadership is learnable. You can do this! Leadership is an observable pattern of practices and behaviors, a definable set of skills and abilities. Any skill can be learned, strengthened, honed, and enhanced, given the motivation and desire, along with practice, feedback, role models, and coaching. When the progress of people who participate in leadership development programs is tracked, the research demonstrates that they improve over time.[1] By learning and practicing, they become better leaders.

The best leaders bring out the best in others.

Here is your moment of truth. We know with certainty that leadership can be learned. We know, without a doubt, that buyers want sellers to demonstrate leadership. The remaining gap is yours to fill. Not everyone wants to learn, and not all who learn about leadership commit fully and master it. Why? Because becoming the very best requires a strong belief that you can learn and grow, an intense aspiration to excel, the determination to challenge yourself constantly, the recognition that you must engage the support of others, and the devotion to practice deliberately. Learning leadership is an ongoing quest, not one with a finish line.[2]

Leadership, like selling, is often misunderstood. Some believe that you must be a "natural born" leader or seller to succeed. They attribute

> **Leadership is an observable pattern of practices and behaviors, a definable set of skills and abilities.**

the success of exemplary leaders and sellers to inborn personality characteristics. They self-select themselves out of leadership or sales because they mistakenly believe they don't have the charisma, charm, abilities, or perseverance required to excel. Research debunks and refutes these notions. It you want to become exemplary in any field, you have to train hard and put in extra effort to practice and hone your skills. This is true in sales. It's also true in leadership. As the old saying goes: *Hard work beats talent when talent doesn't work hard.*

Florida State University professor and noted authority on expertise K. Anders Ericsson made this same point when he said:

Until most individuals recognize that sustained training and effort is a prerequisite for reaching expert levels of performance, they will continue to misattribute lesser achievement to the lack of natural gifts, and will thus fail to reach their own potential.[3]

Decades of research reveal that raw talent is not all there is to becoming a top performer. "One of the first things you learn when you study achievement for a living," says Heidi Grant Halvorson, associate director of the Motivation Science Center at Columbia University, "is that innate ability (to the extent there is such a thing) tells you nothing about your chances of reaching a goal."[4] Talent is not the key that unlocks excellence.

In sales, top performers aren't necessarily the ones with the highest IQs or the most experience. In fact, experience can be a barrier to performance if you are trapped in old ways of doing things. Being the best, in any field, requires deliberate practice. Practicing *deliberately* doesn't mean you engage in selling activities and leadership behaviors as they present themselves to you. Instead, you engage in experiences designed specifically to improve performance. "Designed" is the key idea, meaning there's a methodology and a specific goal involved. Second, practice is not a one-time event. It's not limited to the occasional role play in sales training or to four-legged coaching calls with your sales manager. Engaging in a designed learning experience is something you must do over and over again, until the behavior you're learning becomes automatic. That takes hours of repetition.

Deliberate practice also involves getting feedback. You won't know how well you're doing if you don't have a coach, mentor, manager, colleague, or buyer analyzing and evaluating your performance. When you're mastering a new skill or developing a new habit, it's virtually impossible to assess your own performance.

Deliberate practice isn't much fun. What keeps top performers going during grueling practice sessions is not their enjoyment of that activity, but the knowledge that they are improving and getting closer to their dream of superior performance when it counts.

Last but not least, practice takes time. The more you practice selling skills, the better you become in demonstrating expertise with each skill you've honed. Leadership is no different. To become an exemplary leader, make learning leadership a daily habit. You must commit to practicing leadership with buyers in every encounter. You have to make choices to lead your internal partners. To lead, you must engage in leadership behaviors more often.

> **Being the best, in any field, requires deliberate practice.**

You won't ever be 100 percent perfect, and certainly not on day one. That's okay. Buyers in our research rated the frequency of behaviors, not their quality. They just want to see sellers utilizing leadership behaviors more often. With dedicated practice on your leadership, quality will naturally develop. Don't wait until you've mastered a leadership practice before you demonstrate it to your buyers. Instead, practice every day with your buyers. They will notice and respond favorably to the behaviors themselves and in this way you will be differentiated from other sellers.

As you step into your role as a leader with your buyers, there's one more thing to work on. It's a big one. *You must also lead yourself.*

The instrument of leadership is the self. Mastery of the art of leadership comes from mastery of the self. Engineers have computers, painters have canvas and brushes, musicians have instruments, and sellers have products and services. Leaders have only themselves. Becoming the best leader you can be means becoming the best self you can be. Therefore, leadership development is fundamentally self-development.

Self-development makes you more than a seller with a product to sell. It gives you confidence in you—and this confidence is infectious, making buyers believe in you. The better you know yourself, the better you can make sense of the often incomprehensible and conflicting messages you receive daily. Sell this, sell that. Pitch this, pitch that. Change this, change that. You need internal guidance to navigate the turmoil in today's highly uncertain environment. The internal compass you need comes from understanding yourself and what you value, why you value it, and what actions you can take to back up what you believe. From this self-development comes self-assuredness and, in turn, an ability to inspire others. The confidence that others have in you gives you the latitude to challenge your buyers' status quo. It makes it possible for you to support buyers in ways that allow them to participate in creating what they want.

Learning about yourself and about leadership gives you a strong start. But deciding to be an exemplary leader is not the same as *being* one. Leading is *doing*. It's making behavioral choices in everything you do. You need to do something every day to learn more about leading, and you need to put those lessons into practice daily.

The instrument of leadership is the self. Mastery of the art of leadership comes from mastery of the self.

Leadership happens in the moment. There are many moments with buyers each day when you can choose to lead. In those interactions you can choose to do small things that will make a difference. Each day you can choose to lead by your example. Each day you can choose to lift the spirits of your buyers. Each day you can choose to find exciting opportunities for your buyers. Each day you can choose to strengthen the relationships you have with your buyers. Each day you can choose to say "thank you" more often.

Start leading. The more frequently you choose to lead, the more you will create those awesome connecting experiences that make extraordinary things happen.

> **Leading is *doing*. It's making behavioral choices in everything you do.**

SOURCES AND NOTES

Introduction: How You Make Extraordinary Sales Happen

1 J.M. Kouzes and B.Z. Posner, *The Leadership Challenge: How to Make Extraordinary Things Happen in Organizations*, 6th ed. (Hoboken, NJ: John Wiley & Sons, 2017).

2 Ibid.

Chapter 1: When Sellers Are at Their Best

1 All of the case studies discussed in this book are of actual sellers and buyers. We are indebted to them for their willingness to share with us and others their experiences and stories.

2 Quotations without personal attribution are verbatim comments from our research made by buyers and sellers who anonymously completed various research surveys and questionnaires.

3 R. Lewis and M. Dart, *The New Rules of Retail: Competing in the World's Toughest Marketplace* (New York: Palgrave Macmillan, 2014), 90.

4 A. Iannarino, *The Only Sales Guide You'll Ever Need* (New York: Portfolio/Penguin, 2016), 44, 50.

5 J. Blount, *Sales EQ* (Hoboken, NJ: John Wiley & Sons, 2017), 169.

6 L. Richardson, *Changing the Sales Conversation* (New York: McGraw-Hill, 2014), 142–143.

7 B.J. Pine II and J.H. Gilmore, *The Experience Economy* (Boston: Harvard Business Review Press, 2011), 110–111.

8 B.J. Pine II, and J.H. Gilmore, *Authenticity* (Boston: Harvard Business Review Press, 2007), 150.

9 C.K. Prahalad and V. Ramaswamy, *The Future of Competition: Co-Creating Unique Value with Customers* (Boston: Harvard Business School, 2004), 16–17.

10 R. Lewis and M. Dart, *The New Rules of Retail*, 66.

11 E. Kolsky, "50 Important Customer Experience Stats for Business-Leaders," HuffPost, October 15, 2015, updated October 15, 2016, http://www.huffingtonpost.com/vala-afshar/50-important -customer-exp_b_8295772.html.

12 J.M. Kouzes and B.Z. Posner, *The Leadership Challenge: Making Extraordinary Things Happen in Organizations*, 6th ed. (Hoboken, NJ: John Wiley & Sons, 2017).

13 For detailed information on this research methodology, the theory and evidence behind The Five Practices of Exemplary Leadership® and the *Leadership Practices Inventory*, see B. Posner, "Bringing Rigor of Research to the Art of Leadership," http://www.leadershipchallenge.com/Research-section-Our-Authors -Research-Detail/bringing-the-rigor-of-research-to-the-art-of -leadership.aspx.

14 Gartner Research, CEB Analysis, The New Normal in B2B Sales and Marketing: Customer Dysfunction, infographic, 2017.

Chapter 2: Credibility Is the Foundation of Both Leadership and Making the Sale

1 The classic study on credibility goes back to C.I. Hovland, I.L. Janis, and H.H. Kelley, *Communication and Persuasion* (New

Haven, CT: Yale University Press, 1953); early measurement studies include J.C. McCroskey, "Scales for the Measurement of Ethos," *Speech Monographs 33*, 1966, 65–72; and D.K. Berlo, J.B. Lemert, and R.J. Mertiz, "Dimensions for Evaluation the Acceptability of Message Sources," *Public Opinion Quarterly 3*, 1969, 563–576. Also see D.J. O'Keefe, *Persuasion: Theory and Research* 3rd ed. (Thousand Oaks, CA: Sage, 2016), and R. Cialdini, *Influence: The Psychology of Persuasion* (New York: Collins, 2007).

2 J.M. Kouzes and B.Z. Posner, *Credibility*, 2nd ed. (San Francisco: John Wiley & Sons, 2011), 16–17.

3 J.M. Kouzes and B.Z. Posner, *Credibility*, xv–xvi.

4 J.W. Gardner, *On Leadership* (New York: Free Press, 1990), 28–29.

5 J.M. Kouzes and B.Z. Posner, *The Leadership Challenge: Making Extraordinary Things Happen in Organizations,* 6th ed. (Hoboken, NJ: John Wiley & Sons, 2017), 31.

Chapter 3: Clarify Values

1 J.M. Kouzes and B.Z. Posner, *The Leadership Challenge: Making Extraordinary Things Happen in Organizations,* 6th ed. (Hoboken, NJ: John Wiley & Sons, 2017), 29–33.

2 C.H. Green, *Trust-Based Selling* (New York: McGraw-Hill, 2006), 5–6, 20–22, 45.

Chapter 4: Set the Example

1 Richardson, 2016 Selling Challenges Study, 3.

2 D. Calvert, *DISCOVER Questions Get You Connected for Professional Sellers* (San Jose, CA: Winston Keen James, 2013), 116–123.

3 D. Calvert, *DISCOVER Questions,* 136.

4 J.M. Kouzes and B.Z. Posner, *The Truth About Leadership: The No-Fads, Heart-of-the-Matter Facts You Need to Know* (San Francisco: Jossey-Bass, 2010), 119.

5   S. Callahan, *Putting Stories to Work: Mastering Business Storytelling* (Melbourne, Australia: Pepperberg Press, 2016).

Chapter 5: Envision the Future

1   S. Iyengar and M. Lepper, "When Choice Is Demotivating: Can One Desire Too Much of a Good Thing?" *Journal of Personality and Social Psychology*, 79(6), 2000, 995–1006.

2   A. Duckworth, *Grit* (New York: Simon & Schuster, 2016), 57–58.

3   J.M. Kouzes and B.Z. Posner, "To Lead, Create a Shared Vision," *Harvard Business Review,* January 2009, 20–21.

4   S. Castleberry and D. Shepherd, "Effective Interpersonal Listening and Personal Selling," *Journal of Personal Selling and Sales Management, 13*(1), 2013, 35–49.

5   R. Ramsey and R. Sohi, "Listening to Your Customers: The Impact of Perceived Salesperson Listening Behaviors on Relational Outcomes," *Journal of the Academy of Marketing Science, 25*(2), 1997, 127–137.

6   P.J. Palmer, *Let Your Life Speak* (San Francisco: Jossey-Bass, 2000).

Chapter 6: Enlist Others

1   In a similar way, Simon Sinek talks about how people can be inspired by starting with "why." See S. Sinek, *Start with Why: How Great Leaders Inspire Everyone to Take Action* (New York: Portfolio, 2010).

2   F. Randall and D. Randall, *History of the Development of Building Construction in Chicago* (Urbana: University of Illinois Press, 1999), 286.

3   M. Benioff, *Behind the Cloud: The Untold Story of How Salesforce. com Went from Idea to Billion-Dollar Company and Revolutionized an Industry* (San Francisco: Jossey-Bass, 2009), 44.

4   J. Geary, *I Is an Other: The Secret Life of Metaphor and How It Shapes the Way We See the World* (New York: HarperCollins, 2011), 5.

5   J. Bruner, *Actual Minds, Possible Worlds* (Cambridge, MA: Harvard University Press, 1985).

6   G. Sparks, "Charismatic Leadership: Findings of an Exploratory Investigation of the Techniques of Influence," *Journal of Behavioral Studies in Business, 7*, September 2014.

Chapter 7: Search for Opportunities

1   E. Collins, "B2B Loyalty, The B2C Way," Forrester Research., *Inc.*, March 19, 2015, 2–4.

2   M. Dixon and B. Adamson, *The Challenger Sale: Taking Control of the Customer Conversation* (New York: Penguin Group, 2011).

3   M. Dixon and B. Adamson, *The Challenger Sale,* 18.

4   S. Plous, *The Psychology of Judgment and Decision Making* (New York: McGraw-Hill, 1993), 233.

5   A. Koriat, S. Lichtenstein, and B. Fischhoff, "Reasons for Confidence," *Journal of Experimental Psychology: Human Learning and Memory 6,* 1980, 107–118.

6   L. Thurstone, *The Nature of Intelligence* (London: Routledge & Kegan Paul, 1924).

7   A. Grant, *Originals: How Non-Conformists Move the World* (New York: Viking, 2016), 7.

Chapter 8: Experiment and Take Risks

1   K.E. Weick, "Small Wins: Redefining the Scale of Social Problems," *American Psychologist, 39*(1), 1984, 43.

2   S.R. Maddi, *Hardiness: Turning Stressful Circumstances into Resilient Growth* (New York: Springer, 2013).

3 P.T. Bartone, "Resilience Under Military Operational Stress: Can Leaders Influence Hardiness?" *Military Psychology 18*, 2006, S141–S148.

4 C.S. Dweck, *Mindset: The New Psychology of Success* (New York: Random House, 2006), 6–7.

5 L.M. Brown and B.Z. Posner, "Exploring the Relationship Between Learning and Leadership," *Leadership & Organization Development Journal, 22*(6), 2001, 274–280.

6 K. De Meuse, G. Dia, and G. Hallenbeck, "Learning Agility: A Construct Whose Time Has Come," *Consulting Psychology Journal: Practice and Research, 62*(2), 2010, 1.

Chapter 9: Foster Collaboration

1 K.M. Newman, "Why Cynicism Can Hold You Back," *Greater Good*, June 11, 2015, http://greatergood.berkeley.edu/article/item/why_cynicism_can_hold_you_back.

2 B.A. De-Jong, K.T. Dirks, and N. Gillespie, "Trust and Team Performance: A Meta-Analysis of Main Effects, Moderators, and Covariates," *Journal of Applied Psychology, 101*(8), 2016, 1134–1150.

3 T. Jackson, "Driving for Dollars: Salesmen Think Buyers Lie," *Bankrate*, March 17, 2017, http://www.bankrate.com/auto/driving-for-dollars-salesmen-think-buyers-lie/.

4 P.S. Schockley-Zalabak, S. Morreale, and M. Hackman, *Building the High-Trust Organization: Strategies for Supporting Five Key Dimensions of Trust* (San Francisco: Jossey-Bass, 2010).

5 D. Calvert, *DISCOVER Questions® Get You Connected for Professional Sellers* (Morgan Hill. CA: Winston Keen James, 2013). Field research reported by observing sales coaches and interviews with buyers and sellers from 2003–2013.

6 M. Mortensen and T. Neeley, "Reflected Knowledge and Trust in Global Collaboration," *Management Science, 58*(12), December 2013, 2207–2224.

7 M. An, *Buyers Speak Out: How Sales Needs Evolve* (HubSpot Sales Perceptions Study 2016), April 6, 2017, https://research.hubspot .com/buyers-speak-out-how-sales-needs-to-evolve

8 D. Cohen and L. Prusak, *In Good Company: How Social Capital Makes Organizations Work* (Boston: Harvard Business School Press, 2001), 20; and B.J. Jones, *Social Capital in America: Counting Buried Treasure* (New York: Routledge, 2011).

Chapter 10: Strengthen Others

1 J. Maxfield, "A Lot of Investors Are Still Shorting Chipotle Mexican Grill's Stock," *Motley Fool,* May 14, 2017, http://m .nasdaq.com/article/a-lot-of-investors-are-still-shorting-chipotle -mexican-grills-stock-cm788998.

2 D.K. Srinivasan, "Psychological Ownership: Its Relationship with Interpersonal Trust and Work Outcomes," *Proceedings of the Twelfth AIMS International Conference on Management,* 1501.

3 R.E. Wood and A. Bandura, "Impact of Conceptions of Ability on Self-Regulatory Mechanisms and Complex Decision Making," *Journal of Personality and Social Psychology 56,* 1989, 407–415. See also A. Bandura and R.E. Wood, "Effects of Perceived Controllability and Performance Standards on Self-Regulation of Complex Decision Making," *Journal of Personality and Social Psychology 56,* 1989, 805–814, and A.M. Saks, "Longitudinal Field Investigation of the Moderating and Mediating Effects of Self-Efficacy on the Relationship Between Training and Newcomer Adjustment," *Journal of Applied Psychology 80,* 1995, 211–225.

4 J.M. Kouzes and B.Z. Posner, *Learning Leadership: The Five Fundamentals of Becoming an Exemplary Leader* (San Francisco: The Leadership Challenge–A Wiley Brand, 2016).

5 J. Muir, *The Perfect Close* (Herriman, UT: Best Practice International, 2016), 76, 25.

6 J. Lipsius, *Selling to the Point* (Pacific Palisades, CA: Rydal Road, 2015), 151.

Chapter 11: Recognize Contributions

1 D. Whitney and A. Trosten-Bloom, *The Power of Appreciative Inquiry: A Practice Guide to Positive Change,* 2nd ed. (San Francisco: Berrett-Koehler, 2010); M.E. Seligman, *Flourish: A Visionary New Understanding of Happiness and Well-Being* (New York: Free Press, 2011); and A. Gostick and C. Elton, *All In: How the Best Managers Create a Culture of Belief and Drive Big Results* (New York: Free Press, 2012).

2 A. Fishbach and S.R. Finkelstein, "How Feedback Influences Persistence, Disengagement, and Changes in Goal Pursuit," in H. Aarts and A.J. Ellios (eds.), *Goal-Directed Behavior* (New York: Psychology Press, 2012), 203–230.

3 A. Bryant, *The Corner Office: Indispensable and Unexpected Lessons from CEOs on How to Lead and Succeed* (New York: Times Books, 2011).

4 D. Novak and C. Bourg, *O Great One! A Little Story About the Awesome Power of Recognition* (New York: Penguin Random House, 2016), 210.

5 D. Schwabel, "David Novak: Why Recognition Matters in the Workplace," *Forbes*, May 26, 2016, https://www.forbes.com/sites/danschawbel/2016/05/23/david-novak-why-recognition-matters-in-the-workplace/#3c4037f57bb4.

Chapter 12: Celebrate the Values and Victories

1 See D. Brooks, *The Social Animal: The Hidden Sources of Love, Character, and Achievement* (New York: Random House, 2011).

2 W. Baker, *Achieving Success Through Social Capital: Tapping the Hidden Resources in Your Personal and Business Networks* (San Francisco: Jossey-Bass, 2000); R. Putnam, *Bowling Alone: The*

Collapse and Revival of American Community (New York: Touchstone, 2001); and W. Bolander, C.B. Satornino, D.E. Hughes, and G.R. Ferris, "Social Networks Within Sales Organizations: Their Development and Importance for Salesperson Performance," *Journal of Marketing, 79*(6), 2015, 1–16.

3   T. Deal and M.K. Key, *Corporate Celebration: Play, Purpose, and Profit at Work* (San Francisco: Berrett-Koehler, 1998), 5.

4   C. von Scheve and M. Salmela, *Collective Emotions: Perspectives from Psychology, Philosophy and Sociology* (Oxford, UK: Oxford University Press, 2014).

5   A. Olsson and E.A. Phelps, "Social Learning of Fear," *Nature Neuroscience, 10*(9), 2007, 1095–1102.

6   R. Friedman, *The Best Places to Work: The Art and Science of Creating an Extraordinary Workplace* (New York: Penguin Random House, 2014).

7   M. Csikszentmihalyi, *Finding Flow: The Psychology of Engagement with Everyday Life* (New York: Basic Books, 1998); D. Gilbert, *Stumbling on Happiness* (New York: Knopf, 2006); T. Rath, *Vital Friends: The People You Can't Afford to Live Without* (New York: Gallup Press, 2006); and S. Achor, *Happiness Advantage: The Seven Principles That Fuel Success and Performance at Work* (New York: Crown Business, 2010).

8   C.L. Porath, A. Gerbasi, and S.L. Schorch, "The Effects of Civility on Advice, Leadership, and Performance," *Journal of Applied Psychology, 100*(5), 2015; also see C.L. Porath and A. Gerbasi, "Does Civility Pay?" *Organizational Dynamics 44,* 2015, 281–286.

9   D. Keltner, "Managing Yourself: Don't Let Power Corrupt You," *Harvard Business Review*, October 2016.

10   G. Klein, *The Power of Intuition: How to Use Your Gut Feelings to Make Better Decisions at Work* (New York: Crown Business, 2004), and G. Klein, *Seeing What Others Don't: The Remarkable Ways We Gain Insights* (New York: Penguin, 2013).

Chapter 13: Leadership Is Everyone's Business

1 B.Z. Posner, "A Longitudinal Study Examining Changes in Students' Leadership Behavior," *Journal of College Student Development, 50*(5), 2009, 551–563; and R. Eckert, S. Issakyan, and W. Mulhern, *The Effectiveness of the Leadership Development Programme in Europe* (Greensboro, NC: Center for Creative Leadership, 2014).

2 J.M. Kouzes and B.Z. Posner, *Learning Leadership: The Five Fundamentals of Becoming an Exemplary Leader* (San Francisco: The Leadership Challenge–A Wiley Brand, 2016).

3 K.A. Ericsson, "The Influence of Experience and Deliberate Practice on the Development of Superior Expert Performance," in K.A. Ericsson, N. Charness, P.J. Feltovich, and R.R. Hoffman (eds.), *The Cambridge Handbook of Expertise and Expert Performance* (New York: Cambridge University Press, 2006), 699.

4 H. G. Halvorson, *Succeed: How We Can Reach Our Goals* (New York: Plume/Penguin, 2012), 209.

ACKNOWLEDGMENTS

YOU CAN'T DO IT ALONE, and in keeping with this truth about leadership, we want to take a moment to acknowledge that we couldn't have written this book without support and encouragement from a variety of people. Let's begin with the hundreds of buyers who took the time to complete our surveys, and even more importantly wrote about experiences and insights concerning relationships with sellers and the actions and behaviors that make a difference in their purchase decisions. We also greatly appreciate the scores of sellers, many of them mentioned by name in the text, who also shared with us their experiences, and often frustrations and challenges, in being the best sales person they could be and doing all they could to make their customers and clients successful. The actual experiences and stories of both buyers and sellers provided the impetus for this book and the nuggets about what it takes to make extraordinary things happen. We are also grateful to the community of sales experts, authors, speakers, trainers, podcasters, and organizations who have supported our research and helped to promote this work.

The book you are holding in your hands or reading electronically could not have been produced without the dedicated work of a talented group of people at our publisher, John Wiley & Sons. They deserve a standing ovation. The thanks begin with Jeanenne Ray (editor) and Shannon Vargo (associate publisher), who saw the possibilities of changing the seller/buyer conversation through integrating the concepts associated with The Five Practices of Exemplary Leadership. Other stars on the Wiley team who made a valuable contribution include Danielle Serpica (editorial assistant), Rebecca Taff (copy editor), Carly Hounsome (senior production manager), Dawn Kilgore (senior production editor), and Michael Friedberg (senior marketing manager). A standing ovation also goes out to our friend, colleague, and official developmental editor Leslie Stephen, who brings out the best through her insightful questions, suggestions, and spectacular editing.

Finally, we are most grateful to our spouses and life-time partners: Tae Kouzes, Jackie Schmidt-Posner, and Kinley Calvert. Our thanks to you for your wise advice and counsel, for putting up with us generally, and for giving us the space to work on this book while picking up the slack on other matters that we let slide. You three truly provide an "awesome connecting experience."

ABOUT THE AUTHORS

JIM KOUZES is the Dean's Executive Fellow of Leadership, Leavey School of Business at Santa Clara University, and lectures on leadership around the world to corporations, governments, and nonprofits.

BARRY POSNER holds the Accolti Chair at Santa Clara University, and is Professor of Leadership and the former Dean of the Leavey School of Business. An accomplished scholar, he also provides leadership workshops and seminars worldwide.

Jim and **Barry** are the authors of *The Leadership Challenge, Learning Leadership, Credibility, The Truth About Leadership, A Leader's Legacy, Encouraging the Heart*, and *The Student Leadership Challenge*, among several other best-selling works. They also developed the highly acclaimed *Leadership Practices Inventory* (LPI)®.

DEB CALVERT is the president and founder of People First Productivity Solutions, a consulting and training firm that builds organizational strength by putting people first. Deb's first book, also based on buyer research, was the bestseller *DISCOVER Questions® Get You Connected,* named by HubSpot as one of the Top 20 Most Highly Rated Sales Books of All Time.

Jim Kouzes is a highly regarded leadership scholar and an experienced executive; the *Wall Street Journal* cited him as one of the twelve best executive educators in the United States. Among the many honors that Jim has received are the Thought Leadership Award from the Instructional Systems Association, the most prestigious award given by the trade association of training and development industry providers, the Golden Gavel, the highest honor awarded by Toastmasters International, Trust Across America's Lifetime Achievement award, and has consistently been selected as one of the Top 30 Global Leadership Gurus.

Jim, along with Barry Posner, received the Association for Talent Development's (ATD) highest award for Distinguished Contribution to Workplace Learning and Performance and they have been named Management/Leadership Educators of the Year by the International Management Council; ranked by *Leadership Excellence* magazine in the top twenty on its list of the Top 100 Thought Leaders; named among the 50 Top Coaches in the United States (according to *Coaching for Leadership*); listed among *HR* magazine's Most Influential International Thinkers; and included in the list of "Today's Top 50 Leadership Innovators Changing How We Lead" by *Inc.* magazine.

Jim is a frequent keynote speaker, and has conducted numerous leadership development programs for corporate and for-purpose organizations around the globe. He served as president, CEO, and chairman of the Tom Peters Company from 1988 through 2000, and prior to that led the Executive Development Center at Santa Clara University (1981–1988). Jim founded the Joint Center for Human Services Development at San Jose State University (1972–1980) and was on the staff of the School of Social Work, University of Texas. His career in training and development began in 1969 when he conducted seminars for Community Action Agency staff and volunteers in the War on Poverty. Following graduation from Michigan State University (BA degree with honors in political science), he served as a Peace Corps volunteer (1967–1969). He currently serves on the advisory boards of the Positive Coaching Alliance, the School of Leadership

Studies at Gonzaga University, and Inner Will. Jim can be reached at jim@kouzes.com.

Barry Posner, PhD, holds the Michael J. Accolti, S.J. Chair and is professor of leadership at Santa Clara University, where he also served as dean of the Leavey School of Business for twelve years. He has taught as a distinguished visiting professor at the Hong Kong University of Science and Technology, Sabanci University (Istanbul), and the University of Western Australia. At Santa Clara he has received a number of teaching awards and academic honors. An internationally renowned scholar and educator, Barry has authored or co-authored more than one hundred research and practitioner-focused articles. He currently serves on the editorial advisory board for the *Leadership & Organizational Development Journal* and the *International Journal of Servant-Leadership* and received the Outstanding Scholar Award for Career Achievement from the *Journal of Management Inquiry.*

Barry, with his co-author Jim Kouzes, has written more than twelve books on leadership, including *The Leadership Challenge,* now in its sixth edition, which has sold more than 2.5 million copies worldwide and is available in twenty-two languages. This book has won numerous awards, including the Critics' Choice Award from the nation's book review editors, the James A. Hamilton Hospital Administrators' Book of the Year Award, named a Best Business Book of the Year by *Fast Company,* and continues to be included in *The 100 Best Business Books of All Time.*

Barry received his BA with honors in political science from the University of California, Santa Barbara; his MA in public administration from The Ohio State University; and his PhD in organizational behavior and administrative theory from the University of Massachusetts, Amherst. Having provided workshops and seminars with a wide variety of public- and private-sector organizations worldwide, Barry also works at a strategic level with a number of community-based and professional organizations, having served on the board for Uplift Family Services, Global Women's Leadership Network, American Institute of Architects (AIA), SVCreates, Big Brothers/Big Sisters of Santa Clara

County, Center for Excellence in Nonprofits, Junior Achievement of Silicon Valley and Monterey Bay, Public Allies, San Jose Repertory Theater, and Sigma Phi Epsilon Fraternity. Barry can be reached at bposner@scu.edu.

Deb Calvert is the president and founder of People First Productivity Solutions, a consulting and training firm that builds organizational strength by putting people first. Deb's work includes leadership program design and facilitation, strategic planning with executive teams, team effectiveness work, and sales productivity solutions. Deb is a Certified Master of The Leadership Challenge® and is certified as an Executive Coach by the Center for Executive Coaching and the International Coach Federation.

Deb has been recognized by Treeline as one of the 65 Most Influential Women in Business. She is highly regarded as a thought leader in sales, recognized as a top influencer and blogger to follow by dozens of sales organizations, including Top Sales World, Tenfold, GetApp, LeadFuze, PandaDoc, Nutshell, Rise Global, Geckoboard, and Kast. She has been a contributor to articles and broadcasts for *Selling Power* magazine, Salesforce, HubSpot, SalesPop, *Top Sales World* magazine, Women Sales Pros, *HR* magazine, The Sales Enablement Blog, Sales Hacker, *Sales & Marketing Management,* Pipeliner Sales, New Voice Media, Close.io, *Canvas* magazine, *Realizing Leadership* magazine, MHI, *Thinking Bigger Business* magazine, and more. Additionally, Deb is the founder of The Sales Experts Channel on BrightTALK and teaches the Sales Development Principles course at UC-Berkeley. She travels worldwide, speaking to sales groups and working with sales teams to improve their sales productivity. She has been on-stage at Dreamforce, Inbound, Sales Innovation Expo, Sales 2.0, Outbound, and Apttus Acclerate venues, as well as at association and corporate events. She is a member of the National Speakers Association, Women Sales Pros, and the Sales Tribe Alliance.

Deb previously worked as the sales training director for Knight Ridder, a Fortune 500 media company. She started her sales career at *The Kansas City Star* and graduated from the University of Missouri with a BA in English and journalism. Deb completed the prestigious sales acceleration program at the Kellogg School at Northwestern University. Deb's clients come from all sectors and include global companies like Driscoll's, Berkshire Hathaway, Electronic Arts, Toshiba, Imanami, and Yahoo! as well as universities, media companies, and nonprofits such as Camp Fire, Catholic Charities, the Center for Public Policy and Research, and Uplift Family Services. Deb can be reached at deb.calvert@peoplefirstps.com.

If you're looking for opportunities to make a difference for your buyers or in your organization, we can help. For more about Stop Selling & Start Leading®, visit our website www.stopsellingstartleading.com. There you will find information about presentations for your sales organization or for events and other training opportunities. For leaders throughout your organization, learn more about The Leadership Challenge® Workshop, a unique and intensive program that has served as a catalyst for profound leadership transformations, and The Leadership Practices Inventory®, a 360-assessment for leadership behaviors, by visiting www.theleadershipchallenge.com. For other inquiries, please email Deb Calvert directly at deb.calvert@peoplefirstps.com

Index

Page references followed by *fig* indicate an illustrated figure.